Endorsements

In an age where a rapidly growing number of women are indeed "unhinged," both in the secular culture and in the church, Teresa Skepple's book is a necessary and important corrective. In this beautifully written, engaging work, Teresa brilliantly draws from women in Scripture as negative and positive examples for women today. I highly recommend this book for personal study or women's groups.

Becky Aniol, PhD
Veteran Homeschool Mom, Education Consultant,
and Curriculum Specialist

Teresa Skepple does a brilliant job of presenting the examples of women from the Scriptures that were "unhinged" in their human depravity in comparison with women whose lives were divinely transformed by God's redeeming grace. We live in a culture that is progressing further into feminism, and she affirms to Christian women the need for us to cling to the Truth and be women who walk circumspectly in the Truth. I am thankful that God used this short time she had on this earth, under great duress of cancer, to bring to us an encouraging book on what a transformed life in Christ should look like.

Kari Buice
Pastor's Wife and Veteran Homeschool Mom

Doing a quick word search of the word "unhinged" you'll find many meanings; unstable, deranged, disturbed, mad, and unbalanced. It doesn't take a rocket scientist to see Biblical Womanhood is under attack in our day and women are becoming more and more unhinged, but has it always been this way? Has there always been unhinged women and how can we be unhinged no more? Drawing from women of the Bible Teresa Skepple shows us when it comes to being a woman, there is truly nothing new under sun. Unhinged and hinged alike Teresa shows the devastating consequences of women at war with God and beautiful illustrations of women transformed by God. Rich in Scripture, you'll no doubt find this a wonderful resource for your own godliness and in fulfilling the Titus 2 ministry for discipleship.

Erin Coates
Women's Ministry Director, GraceLife Church

I have known Teresa for about fourteen years. We attended the same church where her husband is the senior pastor. We have worked closely in women's ministry together. I have known nothing other than Teresa being a wonderful woman of God. She is a teacher of the bible. She is a role model for young and old women alike. She has a heart to see women grow in their faith in God. She is modest, kind, compassionate and gracious all rolled up into one. She is very wise and spiritually full. She is someone who I know wants to live a life that pleases God.

This is the second manuscript of Teresa's that I have had the privilege of reading. *Unhinged No More* pulls at the very core of my soul. After reading it, I am more convinced that we as women must stand up and reclaim biblical womanhood. Teresa lays it out with biblical truths and conviction. There is no other way to approach such a sensitive and valuable subject, and Teresa knocks it out of the park!

Unhinged No More reminds me that my mind is a battlefield for the enemy, but I am convinced after reading Teresa's manuscript that we as women need to guard our minds as if our lives depended on it. We must wholeheartedly protect biblical womanhood and never allow it to be misrepresented again. Although we have a hard road ahead of us, Teresa's book has fired me up in a way that I am ready to defend biblical womanhood with everything I have in me. I look forward to studying in more depth *Unhinged No More*!

Tammy R, Grant, MS, LPC, NCC
Supv. Program Specialist, Homeless Program
U.S. Department of Veteran Affairs

Among the many things I truly love about *Unhinged No More* is Teresa's ability to draw me deeper into the stories of the women in the Bible that her book discusses. She uncovers why they are relatable for Christian women today while at the same time staying true to the biblical text and the truths of Scripture. This balanced approach has enriched my understanding of these women, not to mention my appreciation for God's providence in the various outcomes, good or tragic, of their respective stories. Teresa's voice is authentic, easy to follow and loving but also boldly emphatic where it needs to be, which comes from her obvious love for God's Word, her concern for Christian women, and her desire to glorify the Lord by her obedience to His calling. Even though I've been teaching women's bible studies since 2004, I learned some new things myself, and I'm so grateful. *Unhinged No More* couldn't come at a more crucial time for Christian women in our world today. I'm inspired and equipped thanks to this book, and I look forward to utilizing it in my women's bible studies.

Laurel J. Davis
Founder/Teacher, Wisdom's Table Women's Bible Study
Principal, Empathy Editorial

I am fortunate to have received an early copy of *Unhinged No More* by Teresa Skepple. I am fortunate to know Mrs. Skepple and was able to read and evaluate as to the benefit of using this book in both small group and individual settings.

Most important to me is a book's faithfulness to biblical doctrine and principles. With that in mind, *Unhinged No More* considers biblical women and their settings accurately. The passages cited are interpreted correctly without speculation or stretching. Mrs. Skepple has avoided the common problem of synthesizing Scripture to the extent of losing it. The points of instruction and encouragement she makes arise from the text and are not just "generally Christian." Therefore, I believe *Unhinged No More* is solidly founded on Scripture at all points.

Secondly, I am interested in a book's pastoral benefit. I believe *Unhinged No More* will be very helpful in aiding the spiritual growth of Christian women in general. While the book is written to women, it is not more specifically targeted than that. Therefore, it is easily beneficial to women in all stages of life and Christian growth. Mrs. Skepple does not shy away from difficult statements; but they are sincere and medicinal. The book both challenges and encourages women to live increasingly godly lives.

Once published, I plan to use *Unhinged No More* within the ministry of our church. I envision it being a great blessing to our congregation.

Patrick Perkins
Pastor of Christian Education, Berean Bible Baptist Church

WHAT IT MEANS TO BE A
TRANSFORMED WOMAN OF GOD

UNHINGED NO MORE

TERESA L. SKEPPLE

Unhinged No More: Understanding What It Means to Be a Transformed Woman of God
Copyright © 2024 by Teresa Skepple

Published by G3 Press
4979 GA-5
Douglasville, GA 30135
www.G3Min.org

All rights reserved. No part of this publication may be reproduced, stored in a retrieval system, or transmitted in any form by any means, electronic, mechanical, photocopy, recording, or otherwise, without prior permission of the publisher, except as provided for by USA copyright law.

Scripture quotations are from the New American Standard Bible (NASB). All emphases in Scripture quotations have been added by the author.

Edited by Laurel J. Davis, Principal, Empathy Editorial

Printed in the United States of America by Graphic Response, Atlanta, GA.

ISBN: 978-1-959908-24-1

Dedication

To My Mother,
Who taught me what a transformed woman of God looks like.

To my Lord and Savior, Jesus Christ,
Who enabled me to keep writing after receiving a devastating diagnosis. I began writing this book in 2018, the same year I was diagnosed with breast cancer. Needless to say, a paradigm shift occurred like never before and my writing was tossed aside. I found myself slipping ever so quickly into discouragement and despair. But God! Without an intimate, personal relationship with Jesus, I know I would be floundering around trying to make sense of my life and the unwanted circumstance that had come upon me.

As the Lord graciously and lovingly brought to my mind His reassuring and encouraging Word, I continued writing what He filled my heart to say. As I wrote, I prayed that His thoughts and all that He wanted to convey would be communicated.

Some of us wonder where God is when bad things happen. Well, God is where He always is. He is high and lifted up, and yet He dwells among the lowly and contrite (Isa 57:15). He is an ever-present help in times of trouble (Ps 46:1). He is daily bearing our burdens (Ps 68:19), and He is a friend who sticks closer than a brother (Prov 18:24).

One of the first Scriptures God brought to my mind after hearing the diagnosis was, "Do not fear, for I am with you; Do not be afraid, for I am your God. I will strengthen you, I will also help you, I will also uphold you with My righteous right hand" (Isa 41:10).

Then He brought one of my favorite Scriptures front and center to mind: "Behold, I have inscribed you on the palms of My hands; your walls are continually before Me" (Isa 49:16).

It is comforting to know that God never takes His eyes off of me. I know that without His transformational work in my life, and direct intervention, I would be curled up in a corner letting life pass me by. My prayer, dear sister, is that you will be equipped, encouraged, and challenged to live a transformed life regardless of the circumstances you face. I pray that *Unhinged No More* will help you understand what it means to be a transformed woman of God. For His glory!

Acknowledgements

Special words of thanks go to:

Jenelle Davis
Thank you for your encouraging words and advice. I am forever grateful to you for giving of your precious time to read through the first half of my manuscript. With six children at the time, homeschooling and managing all of your duties as a wife, you are truly amazing, a modern Proverbs 31 woman.

Pastor Patrick Perkins
Thank you for being so willing to read through my manuscript and for investing so much of your time and wisdom in helping me complete this book. Your biblical prowess is evident to anyone who has heard you teach.

Roger W. F. Skepple
Thank you, my wonderful husband. Your biblical and scholarly wisdom, insight and understanding has guided me every step of the way in writing *Unhinged No More*. My relationship with the Lord and my growth in Him would not be what it is today without you.

Foreword

In May 1998, Rev. Roger and Teresa Skepple arrived in Atlanta to fill a church's pastorate vacancy. Teresa's passionate commitment to reflect and represent the full counsel of God's Word endeared herself in the hearts of the members, especially the women. I found my pastor's wife to be a wise and competent leader, a well-prepared teacher of the Scriptures, and a welcoming friend.

This book, *Unhinged No More,* represents her long-held desire to equip younger and older women with a resource on biblical womanhood. It provides illustrations from the Bible of the failure of "the unhinged woman" compared against the responsive "transformed woman."

If we are honest, there exists today an undeniable thirst for unadulterated truth that is both unchangeable and transformative. The clear-minded woman seeks not a truth that is unsettling as quicksand, or unsteady as the shifting winds, or drowning in shallow waters. *Unhinged No More* clearly provokes us to know the truth of God's divine work, His divine hope, His divine favor, His divine devotion, His divine mandate.

> For whatever was written in former days was written for our instruction, that through endurance and through the encouragement of the scriptures we might have hope. (Rom 15:4)

I am a grandmother of five adorable young girls, ages 11 years to 15. Sister Teresa's writing style, content and end chapter "thought questions" lend itself applicable for my girls. I am hopeful that *Unhinged No More* will prepare them to know God's design for them.

Karen Loritts
Teacher, Speaker
Author, *Beyond Our Generation*

Table of Contents

Endorsements .... *i*
Dedication .... *vii*
Acknowledgements .... *ix*
Foreword .... *xi*

Preface 1
Introduction 7

PART I – UNHINGED WOMEN 19
Chapter 1 – Eve: A Rogue Conversation 21
Chapter 2 – EVE 2.0: A Rogue State of Mind 33
Chapter 3 – Delilah: A Rogue Relationship 49
Chapter 4 – The Adulterous Wife: A Rogue Encounter 67
Chapter 5 – Jezebel and Athaliah: A Royal Rogue Empire 85

PART II – TRANSFORMED WOMEN 101
Chapter 6 – The Samaritan Woman: A Divine Work 103
Chapter 7 – Hannah: A Divine Hope 125
Chapter 8 – Esther: A Divine Favor 143
Chapter 9 – Ruth: A Divine Love 167
Chapter 10 – The Titus 2 Woman: A Divine Mandate 193

Appendix - Three Reasons the Pulpit is No Place for Women 219

Preface

As I stood next to my handsome, six-foot-four father, the wooden double doors swung open, and my uncle began playing that familiar tune on the organ. One glance at all the big smiles on the faces of those gathered on both sides of the aisle—family, friends, co-workers, neighbors, acquaintances and soon-to-be relatives I hadn't met yet—calmed the butterflies wreaking havoc in my stomach. My father, holding me close, took the first step as he led me down the aisle of the historic church that was like a second home to me as far back as I could remember. You could say I started attending that church before I was born.

The look on Roger's face the moment he first saw me was priceless.

"Who gives this woman to be married to this man?" asked Pastor Briscoe. "Her mother and I," my dad responded. With tears in his eyes, my wonderful husband-to-be came to me, took my hand in his, and brought me to where he had been waiting for me. Together we promised "to have and to hold, from this day forth, in sickness and in health, for richer or for poorer, till death do us part." And as they say, the rest is history.

I love going to weddings. Attending a wedding is one of the high points of my entire year. The beautiful bride, the music, the ceremony, and most of all of course, the beautiful couple beginning their new life together: the groom vowing to love, honor, cherish, and protect his wife, and the bride vowing to love, honor, respect, and submit to her husband.

The year 2018 was very special, not because I was invited to a wedding but because I was *in* a wedding. In June of that year, my youngest daughter, Sarah, was united in holy matrimony to her longtime friend, Lucas Pass. God's blessings overflowed in abundance, and Roger and I could hardly contain ourselves. It was the most beautiful ceremony that always puts a big smile on our faces every time we reminisce about it, which is often!

The very first wedding in the history of mankind took place not in a church but in a garden. There was no pastor, no admiring guests smiling at the bride as she walked down the aisle and no flower girl or ringbearer running ahead announcing, "The bride is coming! The bride is coming!" No music was playing in the background, no candles flickering on an altar, no rehearsed ceremony, and no exchanging of vows.

And, at this very first wedding, there was no father of the bride to escort his beautifully adorned daughter down an aisle to her husband-to-be — other than God Himself! Wow! Among Eve's many unique experiences, this one has to be at the top of the list. God the Father brought His daughter Eve and gave her to Adam, and the institution we call marriage was immediately established. Take notice of what the Bible says:

> The Lord God fashioned into a woman the rib which He had taken from the man, and brought her to the man. (Gen 2:22)

We are not told if Adam had tears in his eyes at the first sight of his bride, but we are told what he was thinking. Adam was no doubt ecstatically overwhelmed with joy and gratitude to God for bringing him someone just like him. Out of all of God's creation, there was finally a creation made just for him. Someone he could relate to, talk to and walk through life with, someone beautiful and perfectly suited just for him, who corresponded to him in every way. No more trying to commune with animals. A suitable and exquisite fellow human being was right before him, different from him but like him. God's final creation.

The Apostle Paul articulates God's design of the husband-and-wife relationship this way:

> For a man ought not to have his head covered, since he is the image and glory of God; but the woman is the glory of man. (I Cor 11:7)

In other words, Eve showed off God's "mankind" creation to the fullest, most complete extent.

It might be tempting to think God simply outdid Himself when He created Eve. However, God is perfect, and all that He does is also perfect. To say that God can outdo Himself is to say that God can improve. Yet, creation is another reflection of His absolute perfection! As Adam was the glory of God, Eve was the glory of the man.

I wonder if Adam's emotions began to soar within him at the very sight of his glorious bride. Fully captivated with his lovely wife and realizing that he had in Eve more than he could have ever thought or imagined, the whole scene must have been an incredible moment for him. I can imagine his reaction was, like Roger's, priceless. Adam took one look at Eve and declared:

> This is now bone of my bones, and flesh of my flesh; she shall be called woman, because she was taken out of man. (Gen 2:23)

Unfortunately, that glorious scene was soon shattered after Satan entered the garden in the form of a snake. That calculating serpent, described in the Bible as "more crafty than any beast of the field" (Gen 3:1), interrupted the magnificence of this perfect couple and their perfect home.

It all started with a question. One question was asked and from that moment on, life for Adam and Eve drastically changed.

Several millennia later, another fateful question was asked, this time by a woman, that drastically changed the lives of thousands and thousands of women. This question challenged women to rethink their view on what it means to be productive as a woman. It exhorted women to equate productiveness with personal value, meaning you have no value unless you are productive in the world's evaluation. This question also encouraged women to realize their potential and pursue what the world would say are our higher purposes in life. The woman credited with causing such a massive change in women's lives was Betty Friedan. Her question was, simply, "Is this all?"

In her book, *The Feminine Mystique*, Friedan had the following to say about what she believed was in the heart and soul of every American woman:

> The problem lay buried, unspoken for many years in the minds of American women. It was a strange stirring, a sense of dissatisfaction, a yearning that women suffered in the middle of the twentieth century in the United States. Each suburban housewife struggled with it alone. As she made the beds, shopped for groceries, matched slipcover material, ate peanut butter sandwiches with her children, chauffeured Cub Scouts and Brownies, lay beside her husband at night, she was afraid to ask even of herself the silent question — "Is this all?"[1]

Dissatisfaction breeds dissatisfaction. It would seem Friedan's diagnosis of the state of women "in the middle of the twentieth century in the United States" was actually spot on. Her book, which was published in 1963, reportedly sold nearly three million copies in its first three years of publication. Apparently, her topic and opinion resonated with women. The "strange stirring" that women from all walks of life allegedly were feeling had finally been realized and there was going to be no turning back.

---

[1] Betty Friedan, *The Feminine Mystique* (New York: W. W. Norton & Company, 1963), 57.

In the pages that follow in *Unhinged No More*, we will look more closely at Eve and will see that, at some point, Eve became dissatisfied. She became dissatisfied with her life as she saw it. Her dissatisfaction, like Mrs. Friedan's and countless other women, led her to draw conclusions about herself. It led her to draw conclusions about what would satisfy her moving forward.

We will see that Eve became enamored with a particular tree in the garden of Eden and what it could do for her. Sadly, that tree, rather than God, became the sole answer to her dissatisfaction. It became for her the means to her obtaining the life she thought she could have. But what Eve really needed was what this book is about: transformation.

While dissatisfaction in and of itself is not sinful, a transformed woman of God will process her dissatisfaction through the filter of Scripture. As she obeys Scripture, her dissatisfaction is addressed biblically as she strives to honor God.

I am so glad that you have decided to join me in learning about and understanding what a transformed woman of God looks like. How does she think? How does she talk? How does she behave? How does she dress? What does she value in life? Where do her priorities lie? From where does she receive instruction for living life? What kind of legacy does she build?

There's something to be said about a woman who examines the Word of God and then brings her thoughts, emotions, desires, and longings into conformity with what thus says the Lord. There's something to be said about a woman who works in uniformity with God in fulfilling His agenda for her life. There's something to be said about a woman who intentionally lives for the glory of God, pointing others to Christ.

Transformation is radical. Transformation is real. It leaves nothing in your life untouched. You will never be the same because of it. You will want more and more of it. When you think about transformation, two things should come to mind. First is the work God must do to take you out of the kingdom of darkness and place you into the kingdom of His dear Son (salvation). Second is the work God must do in your life to mature you (sanctification). In other words, transformation starts and continues with God.

While the work of salvation happens in an instant, the work of sanctification takes a lifetime. Let me make this clear, salvation is a work of God alone. He moves in your heart, opens your eyes, causes you to see that you are a sinner in need of a Savior. He gives you repentance and faith, resulting in you believing in Him. You respond to His work in obedience and are saved from His wrath. Sanctification is subsequent and is an ongoing process whereby God allows and enables you to work with Him in your maturation process. God is sovereign and therefore has established your days and set your life in motion. He has determined every circumstance, pleasant and unpleasant, that you will experience. He alone causes the good, the bad, the ugly, and the unexplainable to work according to His will and purpose for you. He accomplishes all of this through divine intervention into your life. When God gets involved in your life, everything changes, and you become useful to Him. The fruit you bear as a result of genuine salvation is ultimately His work in your life, and it glorifies Him.

I like what John the Baptist said in just seven words, seven words that speak so powerfully to a transformed life: He must increase, but I must decrease (John 3:30).

Introduction

What do high heels, a pearl necklace, and a just-below-the-knee dress-wearing woman have in common with a tattooed, gun-slinging, boot-wearing and butt-kicking woman? You guessed it, absolutely nothing, except for the fact that both images, though starkly different, have had a profound effect on women and womanhood in America and elsewhere. And let's not forget the images of braless-dancing and contorted twisting and twerking women dominating our music and entertainment industries today. They are also having an effect on women and womanhood.

Why do you think the Super Bowl halftime shows over the past several years have garnered so many viewers? The 2020 Super Bowl halftime show featuring "J. Lo" (Jennifer Lopez) was reportedly viewed by 102 million people. The 2013 halftime show featuring "Queen Bey" (Beyoncé Knowles) was reportedly viewed by 110.8 million. But those numbers are nothing compared to the whopping 143.6 million viewers who watched Janet Jackson's infamous "wardrobe malfunction" during the 2004 halftime show. Sadly, many women, mothers and even grandmothers see J. Lo, Queen Bey and even Janet Jackson as bold, assertive, ideal role models and encourage young girls to aspire to be like them.

It is no surprise that, because of these kinds of images portrayed on TV, in movies, and live on stage, women are often viewed as nothing more than objects of pleasure, here to gratify. Was this part of the "more" that Betty

Friedan envisioned when she asked her question, "Is this all?," back in 1963? Why not? Anything beats sitting around eating peanut butter sandwiches and matching slipcovers. Apparently, womanhood according to Friedan is whatever satisfies you and meets that yearning for "more" deep inside you.

Some thirty-plus years after the publication of Friedan's book, it appears to be true that women have not even *looked* back, much less *turned* back. We have come a very long way from the knee-length dress-wearing woman portrayed by June Cleaver on the old "Leave It to Beaver" television show. Yes, June fit the mold perfectly of what Betty Friedan loathed. June Cleaver was the epitome of what womanhood was supposed to look like. As one of the best-dressed TV housewives, she taught women everything from how to dress, to how to raise two rambunctious boys, to how to keep house — all with elegant grace, contentment, and joy.

Yes indeed, June Cleaver was definitely a force to be reckoned with. I remember watching episodes of her effortlessly running down the steps in heels just in time to greet her husband with a smile as he entered the house from work. She would serve up meals in those heels. She would even wash dishes without getting a single stain on her starched dress or disturbing the pearl necklace hanging just right around her neck. Not even homemade spaghetti sauce or bacon frying in a pan would be a challenge for Mrs. Cleaver and her pristine attire. She was an amazing woman.

However, Mrs. Cleaver was make-believe. Even still, unfortunately, some women found out the hard way that her version of womanhood was unattainable, unrealistic, and ridiculous. Although women may have enjoyed watching the popular sitcom, Mrs. Cleaver's style of womanhood proved to be unappealing.

No Turning Back

Betty Friedan and her question, "Is this all?," helped paved the way for women to finally realize their full potential. We knew we could do anything we wanted to do and be anything we wanted to be.

Soon after, TV shows featuring women right alongside their male counterparts, working a job and making their own money, quickly became very popular. "You're gonna make it after all"[1] was part of the theme song for the "Mary Tyler Moore Show," which debuted in 1970, that spotlighted an empowered, single, career woman in, ironically, the television industry.

TV commercials featured women working outside the home while also taking care of their responsibilities in the home. As the Enjoli perfume ad from the 1970s touted, women were the only ones who could "bring home the bacon, fry it up in a pan" and never let a man forget he's a man. I don't know how many women purchased Enjoli from that commercial, but I can assure you, many, many women were inspired by its other perhaps more dominant message: Women can have it all, get it all, be it all, and do it all!

On the heels of the Enjoli commercial, the movie "9 to 5" debuted in 1980. The twentieth highest grossing comedy film of all time, "9 to 5" was about three courageous women who revolutionized their workplace environment in the face of egotistical misogyny, sexism, and bigotry in the name of gender equality and women's empowerment. Although countless women had already entered the workforce by this time, the movie helped forge an even clearer path and successful transition from home life to office life and beyond.

With the onslaught of reality TV, talk shows, female vigilante movies, motivational speakers, and professional females in every facet of life, women were empowered all the more, and womanhood began to take on a wider and varied meaning. Womanhood has come to be defined as simply tapping into a power that uniquely belongs to you and that can never be taken away from you. It is affirming to yourself and others that you are powerful, worthy and deserving of good things the world offers. As Laura Robert-Rivera once said:

---

[1] Sonny Curtis, "Love is All Around," *Love is All Around* (Glenview, IL: Ovation Records, 1970).

> In a world that labels me, my place and my worth in reference to the men in my life, I believe being a woman means knowing you are not alone; that all around the world, woman are, have and will rise above any definition, using knowledge, strength, confidence, and passion.[2]

Today, motivational speakers and life coach experts make very little if any mention of womanhood and how far we have come as women. Rather, they focus definitively on your inner self, who you are as a person and becoming better at being you. According to the experts, you are not living your fullest until you are living in your "truth." Womanhood is understood to be how you define yourself, which is also called your "truth." As the renowned inspirational speaker, television personality and life coach Iyanla Vanzant has said,

> [A] shift in your consciousness takes place that you can see, feel and experience when you start living the truth of who you are. It is knowing who you are, defining, understanding, valuing and honoring who you are that enables you to be the best version of you. Attempting to live outside of your true worth will cause you to crash and burn.[3]

According to Rebecca McKown, a writer, spiritual life coach, healer, and modern-day mystic, "personal truth" means:

> [T]o live your most truthful self. Inside you is a person waiting to jump out and live in truth and openness. Most of us spend our days living up to expectations and

---

[2] Laura Robert-Rivera, "International Women's Day 2019: 17 Women Share What Womanhood Means to Them" (March 8, 2019): Retrieved from https://www.teenvogue.com/gallery/international-womens-day-2019-what-womanhood-means.

[3] Iyanla Vanzant, "How to Start Living in the Truth of Who You Are" (Hay House, 2018): Retrieved from https://youtu.be/WSm94x6uONc.

definitions. In this way you, me, all of us are living to be someone different than who we truly are. It is time to live your truth and own it.[4]

McKown offers a four-step process to living "your truth." She says you must, step one, "Accept who you are at this moment"; step two, "Acknowledge who you are"; step three, "Define your truth"; and step four, "Live loudly and proudly."[5]

Mentor, teacher, and spiritual guide Dr. Kate Siner had this to say:

> Living your personal truth is the key to success in your personal development. We must connect with our deeper self and uncover our personal truth. When we live an "unconnected life" (that is, unconnected to our deeper self, our core, our personal truth), what we understand to be "our truth" is nothing more than our ego's petulant desires. When we live a connected life, our deep truth guides us to live an aligned life by providing us with signs and signals along the way. Our job is just to listen to these signals and act accordingly. When we do, our life becomes infinitely more fulfilled.[6]

According to Lisa Nichols, author, motivational speaker and life coach, I am a dynamic expression of God on the quest to know and reveal more of my true self. She continues:

> At your core you're light, at your core you're divinity, you're love, you're resilient, you're perseverance, that's your

---

[4] Rebecca McKown, "Step Into Your Truth With These 4 Simple Steps" (September 7, 2014): Retrieved from https://www.huffpost.com/entry/step-into-your-truth-with_b_5564066.
[5] Ibid.
[6] Dr. Kate Siner, "5 Steps for How to Find Your Inner Truth," (August 21, 2017): Retrieved from https://katesiner.com/tag/personal-truth.

truth, that's what is. Your truth is there. The truth is steady, and then you simply choose if you're going to give yourself permission to live in your truth.[7]

Oh my! What a montage of nauseating foolishness and confusion. What you just read from so-called "experts" is exactly what the Apostle Paul meant when he said:

> For even though they knew God, they did not honor Him as God or give thanks but they became futile in their speculations and their foolish heart was darkened. Professing to be wise, they became fools and exchanged the glory of the incorruptible God for an image in the form of corruptible man ... For they exchanged the truth of God for a lie ... (Rom 1:21–23, 25)

Dear sister, there is no such thing as "personal truth" or my truth, your truth, her truth, or his truth. Truth is truth, not because it is yours or mine but because it is God's truth. Truth is truth whether or not you accept it, acknowledge it, understand it or agree with it. Truth is truth regardless of whether it validates your life experiences. A. W. Tozer made it clear when he said, "His words are the essence of truth. He is not offering an opinion, Jesus never uttered opinions. He never guessed; He knew, and He knows."[8]

God's truth entails several realities that we must understand as transformed women of God. These realities include the following:

- God is both the author and foundation of truth. Apart from Him, there is no such thing as truth. (John 14:6; Ps 118:160)

---

[7] Lisa Nichols, "Claiming Truth: Lisa Nichols On the Truth That Resides in Us All," (UnityOnlineOrg, 2020): Retrieved from https://www.youtube.com/watch?v=iDvVWEkUSAo.

[8] A.W. Tozer, *The Pursuit of God* (Ventura, CA: Regal Books, 2013), 100.

- God is sovereign. Everything He says flows from His sovereignty and is absolute, certain, and unchanging. (Ps 33:9)
- Our very existence is predicated on God's truth. (Gen 1:26; Ps 139:15–16)
- God's truth is the only avenue by which we can know Him and through which we are to worship Him. (Ps 43:3; Jas 1:18; John 4:24)
- Through God's truth, we are justified, glorified, and sanctified. (Rom 8:29–30, John 17:17)
- Through God's truth, we become and remain wise. (Ps 19:7)
- Through God's truth, our mind can be transformed and renewed. (Rom 12:1; Phil 4:8)

The only way we can recognize and understand truth is by making the Word of God foundational to our lives. Any belief or "truth" devised outside of or in contradiction to God's Word is simply another avenue to living life in rebellion against God.

God's truth is reality. God's truth matters. "My truth," however, is code for *I act and live and think the way I choose to act and live and think. I am my own person, and no one has the right to tell me how to act, how to think, or how to live my life.* As such, "my truth" is nothing more than individualism that edges out God and His authority. "My truth" is nothing more than my opinion, my likes and dislikes, and my preference. Furthermore, as I grow and learn and develop in my thinking and I am changing as a person in the process, it follows then that "my truth" is also changing instead of being grounded and absolute.

Instead of this way of thinking, what is needed is an objective, unchanging, reliable truth. The objective, unchanging, reliable truth needed is found only in the Lord Jesus Christ. Therefore, a transformed woman of God willingly denies herself, takes up her cross *daily* and follows Christ (Matt 16:24).

Unfortunately, but not surprising, life coach experts refer to the denial of self as hating on yourself. Rather than denying self, they encourage the opposite, namely, *elevating* self. Self should always be front and center so that higher levels of self-awareness can be realized.

God does not save us so we can gain higher levels of self-awareness. Scripture assumes that we have too much self-awareness. Rather, "if anyone thinks he is something when he is nothing, he deceives himself" (Gal 6:3), "for by the grace given to me I say to everyone among you not to think of himself more highly than he ought to think, but to think with sober judgment, each according to the measure of faith that God has assigned" (Rom 12:3).

God does not save just to be in your life. The main reason He saves is to give you the gift of eternal life with Him in heaven. In the meantime, He saves to transform you into the image of His Son, the Lord Jesus Christ. God saves to transform your life to the extent that enables you to live in obedience to His will and purpose, for His glory.

A lot of women these days go around trying to make themselves appear to be living the life. They are trying to capture attention and turn heads. Sadly, they are hurting inside. They are questioning life. They are questioning their purpose. They are unfulfilled women, always looking for more out of life. Following their own desires and agenda has left them exhausted and empty. Solomon calls it "striving after the wind" (Eccl 1:14).

Too many women have simply added God to their lives like a spare tire. He is there for them when they need Him. He is there for them when they need Him to accomplish something they want in life. He is there to champion their cause and to provide a way forward to reach the worldly goals they have set for themselves. He is there to move them out of the way when troubles and trials get too close for comfort. He is in their lives for their every beck and call.

Transformation is a work of God. Transformation happens from the inside out. In their book, *Transformed: Life-Taker to Life-Giver,* Karen

INTRODUCTION

Hodge and Susan Hunt define transformation as "the process whereby the Holy Spirit effects such a radical, revolutionary change in our hearts that it is revealed in our affections, ambitions, actions and attitudes."[9]

Notice the words of the prophet Ezekiel about what happens to every person God transforms:

> Moreover, I will give you a new heart and put a new spirit within you; and I will remove the heart of stone from your flesh and give you a heart of flesh. I will put My Spirit within you and cause you to walk in My statutes and you will be careful to observe My ordinances. (Ezek 36:26–27)

It is God who gives a new heart and a new spirit. It is God who removes the stony heart. It is God who gives a heart of flesh. It is God's Spirit put within you. It is God's statutes in which you are to walk. It is God's ordinances that are to be observed.

When God transforms you, your life is no longer centered on you and "your truth." Your life is consumed with walking in *His* statutes and observing *His* ordinances. Your life and the way you live acknowledges that you are here for God, not for yourself, created to glorify Him, not yourself (Isa 43:7).

Consider the words of a popular chorus originally sung by the Brooklyn Tabernacle Choir. "Made to Live for You" should be the heart-cry of every transformed woman of God:

> I was created for Your glory, Your glory
> All of my days were made for You
> Lord, You have formed me and
> You know me, You know me
> Without You, Lord, what can I do?

---

[9] Karen Hodge and Susan Hunt, *Transformed: Life-Taker to Life-Giver* (Ross-shire, Scotland: Christian Focus, 2016), 12.

I was made to live for You.
I was made to live for You.
Lord, I give my life as a sacrifice for You
I give everything as an offering to You
I was made to live for You
I was made to live for You[10]

No Sugar, No Spice, Everything Naughty, Not Nice

When I was growing up, there was a little rhyme I heard often and eventually memorized. I don't remember exactly when I learned it, but I was exposed to it a lot, usually from older women. Perhaps you know it, as well. It goes like this:

> What are little girls made of?
> Sugar and spice and everything nice,
> That's what little girls are made of.
> Sunshine and rainbows and ribbons for hair bows
> That's what little girls are made of.
> Tea parties, laces and baby doll faces
> That's what little girls are made of.

Unfortunately, the heading above—"No Sugar, No Spice, Everything Naughty, Not Nice"—is the best description for the women I will highlight in Part One of *Unhinged No More*. We will examine the lives of several troubled (unhinged) women in the Bible: an ominous girlfriend, an unfaithful wife, a married woman sexually attracted to her servant, an evil queen, and a murderous grandmother.

The Bible does not tell us anything about their childhood experiences as little girls. It does not tell us how they became the infamous women

---

[10] The Brooklyn Tabernacle Choir, "Made to Live For You," in *Declare Your Name (Live Worship)*. Lyrics retrieved from http://www.songlyrics.com/the-brooklyn-tabernacle-choir/made-to-live-for-you-lyrics.

presented in Scripture. However, as we study their stories, it will become clear that sugar and spice and everything nice was never a part of their DNA. They were women devoid of a transformed life, who embodied destructiveness. Women who were steeped in rebellion and foolishness. Their sinful legacy is on full display on the pages of Scripture. They are unhinged women. Solomon described the unhinged woman as one who "does not ponder the path of life, her ways are unstable and she does not know it" (Prov 5:6).

In Part Two, we will examine the lives of women in the Bible who, in spite of unpleasant situations and numerous struggles, feared God. They will teach us what it means to be a transformed woman of God. They will teach us that being transformed means boldly and courageously living life for the glory of God and not for oneself. Through their authentic displays of wisdom, strength, and humility, these remarkable women will tell us the stories we must hear and are the examples we must follow.

We will conclude our study with the quintessential example of what a transformed woman of God looks like in practical, everyday living from Titus 2. Are you a transformed woman of God? Do you want to be transformed? Keep reading and we will learn together!

> The path of the righteous is like the light of dawn, that shines brighter and brighter until the full day. The way of the wicked is like darkness; they do not know over what they stumble. (Prov 4:18–19)

PART ONE

UNHINGED WOMEN

CHAPTER 1

Eve: A Rogue Conversation
(Genesis 1:26–28; 2:16–18; 3:1–16)

There is a way that seems right to a man,
but its end is the way of death.

Proverbs 16:25

Scripture does not record Eve saying anything at the first sight of Adam, her husband. However, when she spoke, the actions that followed impacted her, her husband, their marriage, the offspring that were yet to come, and, consequently, the entire world.

Now the serpent was more crafty than any beast of the field which the Lord God had made. And he said to the woman, "Indeed, has God said, 'You shall not eat from any tree of the garden'?" The woman said to the serpent, "*From the fruit of the trees of the garden we may eat; but from the fruit of the tree which is in the middle of the garden, God has said, 'You shall not eat from it or touch it, or you will die.'*" The serpent said to the woman, "You surely shall not die! For God knows that in the day you eat from it your eyes will be opened and you will be like God knowing good and evil." When the woman saw that the tree was good for food, and that it was a delight to the eyes, and that the tree was desirable to make one wise, she took from its fruit and ate; and she gave also to her husband with her, and he ate. (Gen 3:1–6, emphasis added)

Did you notice throughout the dialogue that Eve made no appeal to Adam, her husband? Eve said nothing to Adam while conversing with the serpent and made no attempt to bring her husband into the discussion. Notice, too, that the enemy directed his question and comments to Eve alone. Not once did the serpent speak to Adam. Adam was completely excluded from the dialogue; although he could have interjected at any point, he chose to remain silent. As a reader, you are unaware that Adam is "with her" until she gives him the fruit (Gen 3:6). Both the serpent and Eve ignored Adam and ignored the Word of God given by Adam.

Words Matter

In less than forty-five words (vv. 2–3), Eve managed to get herself in a position to be devoured and brought to utter ruin (see 1 Pet 5:8). Because of her words, her desire to have something God never intended for her to have, and her disobedience to God's command, every woman bears the consequence and carries the stigma of her role in the fall of mankind (Gen 3:16; 1 Tim 2:14–15).

As Eve fully absorbed the deceptive words coming from the serpent, her sinful desire was being nurtured along through his manipulation. Then, as the deception took root in her heart, she became convinced that the tree was good for food, was desirable to make one wise, and was aesthetically beautiful (Gen 3:6). It checked all the boxes of a woman's felt needs: security, protection, provision, and beauty, along with the added bonus of wisdom. She also became convinced that eating from the tree would make her like God. Once the serpent stopped talking, Eve was all too ready to sink her teeth into the forbidden fruit and experience the new benefits and pleasures she was convinced would come.

One of the results of deception is living and acting in a false reality. How many women have married a man while ignoring the obvious red flags because she was convinced she could change him? How many women have continued in a relationship with a man that led to marriage because she was convinced he could provide all the "things" she wanted? How many women have found themselves in severe misery because of a decision they made based on faulty information?

One of the clear lessons we learn from Eve is that, when you decide to chart a course of action toward a desired goal that ignores the facts and dismisses the Word of God, you open yourself up for overwhelming harm, failure, and disappointment. Notice the sequence of events that led to Eve's sin:

- Eve conversed with the serpent alone.
- Eve responded to the serpent (albeit in error).
- Eve listened to the serpent.
- Eve thought about the fruit and how it could impact her life.
- Eve desired the fruit.
- Eve bought into the lies of the serpent.
- Eve took the fruit from the forbidden tree.
- Eve ate the fruit.
- Eve gave the fruit to her husband with her and he ate. (Gen 3:6)

This was the collapse of the woman, and consequently, womanhood. Her egregious failure to do what God created her to do started the disintegration of biblical womanhood. She was to be a "helper suitable," but in that moment, she failed God. She failed Adam. She failed herself. She failed her future family. She failed all women. Although there was good and productive use for the fruit on the tree of the knowledge of good and evil, God had said, "you shall not eat" (Gen 2:17).

Now consider what happens next:

> They heard the sound of the Lord God walking in the garden in the cool of the day and the man and his wife hid themselves from the presence of the Lord God among the trees of the garden. Then the Lord God called to the man and said to him, "Where are you?" He said, "I heard the sound of You in the garden and I was afraid because I was naked so I hid myself." And He said, "Who told you that you were naked? Have you eaten from the tree of which I commanded you not to eat?" The man said, "The woman whom You gave to be with me, she gave me from the tree, and I ate." (Gen 3:8–12)

The results are devastating:

- What Eve once experienced with God was abruptly ended (v. 8). Sinful behavior immediately and completely breaks fellowship with God.
- Eve's relationship with God was marked by guilt and shame (v. 8). Sinful behavior ushers in fear and anxiety as the full scope of the damages are realized.
- Eve was betrayed by her own husband (v. 12). Sinful behavior in our most intimate relationships results in the greatest sting.

When God's order of the husband lovingly leading and the wife willingly placing herself under his leadership is reversed, disaster strikes, and blame-shifting inevitably follows. Adam, after not only observing but allowing his wife to be verbally assaulted by the serpent, did not hesitate to blame her for his own sin. Rather than protecting Eve and taking some of the responsibility, he threw her under the bus.

Eve's desire to eat from the forbidden tree revealed a deeper issue, which God highlighted when He judged her for her sin: "I will greatly multiply your pain in childbirth. In pain you shall bring forth children; yet your desire shall be for your husband, and he shall rule over you" (Genesis 3:16).

God ordained two judgments on Eve in verse 16. One involved childbirth and also child-rearing. The other had to do with the relationship between her and Adam.

Notice, God judged Eve in the area in which she was to function. God judged her in bearing children, one of the reasons for which she was created. This was why Adam needed a "suitable" helper. Without Eve, Adam could not fulfill God's command in its entirety. This is also one of the reasons why God said, "It is not good for the man to be alone; I will make him a helper suitable" (Gen 2:18). God's judgment was specific and particular. He chose an area of a woman's life where she would severely feel the impact of her sin against Him.

Next, God judged Eve in her marriage relationship. When He said, "Yet your desire shall be for your husband," He was targeting the very core cause in Eve's downfall. Eve chose to take the reins of leadership from Adam and thereby led her family into sin. She made the decision that the family would believe and act upon the serpent's suggestions rather than obey the command of God.

In verse 16, the word "desire" is not sexual desire as some erroneously think. It means taking for yourself a role that was meant for another. Eve took on Adam's role even as he abdicated it. As a result of God's judgment on Eve, a wife would now want ("desire") what was given to her husband to do and to be. She would now be much more inclined to usurp her husband's authority in order to call the shots. Yet, her actions would be met head on with resistance from her husband—"and he shall rule over you."

Consider Eve's desires for a moment, her desire to lead, her desire to make the decisions for the family, her desire not to be accountable to anyone but herself. They are what helped to mislead her in the conversation with the serpent. We need to recognize our tendency towards these same desires and tenaciously work to overcome them.

The judgment God leveled against Eve exacerbated her desire. It also caused her to no longer desire her God-given role of being a suitable helper. It created an environment in which women will always be reminded that marital harmony will be extremely difficult, if not borderline impossible, without Jesus Christ.

When you think about it, many times the conflicts we as women have in our marriages stem from the fact that we want to be the one who makes the decisions. We are presented with various situations at various times in our life, and we take it upon ourselves to figure out how it should be handled. We are ready to settle the matter and move on. However, our husbands may have something different in mind to handle the situation. And the struggle ensues!

Watch Over Your Heart

Your heart cannot be trusted, which is one reason the Bible warns that we are to keep diligent watch over it. The heart is the center of your emotions and desires. Because you are changing, evolving and maturing as a person, your heart is also changing, evolving, and maturing. While Eve initially seemed to have a very stern position against eating from the forbidden tree, something took place in her heart that caused her to desire what was off limits, brought on through deception. Her emotions and feelings then conformed to that desire, enabling her to partake.

"Fiercely guard" is the connotation of what Solomon was conveying when he said, "Watch over your heart with all diligence, for from it flow the issues of life" (Prov 4:23). Many of us go to great lengths to guard our houses and property, but sadly, don't go nearly as far to guard our minds, thoughts, and emotions.

For example, many people not only have locks on their doors, but they also have deadbolt locks. Many people not only have a security system, but they also have surveillance cameras both inside and outside their homes. With the advancement of technology, you can receive a notification to your cell phone the moment someone comes on your property and approaches the front door. Though you may be miles away, you are not only able to see the person on camera, but you can also communicate with them through your phone.

Why do we go to such lengths to protect our place of residence? Why do we "fiercely guard" our property? Because, aside from the fact that it is one of the most valuable assets we own, it provides safety, security and protection to our loved ones. Not everybody is welcomed on our property, and certainly not in our house.

How much more should we fiercely guard our hearts and minds? Every thought, idea or imagination should not be welcomed in your mind. Every dream, ideology, feeling, and conviction should not take up residence in your mind.

Eve allowed her thoughts and emotions to be hijacked by a bold-faced lie (Gen 3:4). She may have had a strong conviction to eat from the tree when she reached for its fruit. However, just because you have a strong conviction about something does not make it right to pursue it.

We are told in the New Testament to take our thoughts captive to the obedience of Christ (2 Cor 10:5). We are to fiercely guard our minds so that, when a thought contrary to the Word of God attempts to take up residence, we capture, examine, and aggressively reject it. What started Eve's demise was her unchecked heart and mind. Yes, Satan played a huge role, but Eve allowed her desires to ultimately control her heart, which in turn led her to do the very thing God had said not to do (Gen 2:16–17; 3:6).

What was true then is still true to this day. If not aligned with God's Word, my dear sister, your inner desires and longings and even convictions will become the start of your demise physically, emotionally, and spiritually. How different the story might have been if Eve had valued God's Word. How different the story might have been if Eve had valued the purpose for which God created her ("helper suitable") more than she valued the personal appeal and usefulness of the fruit. How different the story might have been if Eve had desired for herself what God desired for her.

Such a desire was found in Hannah when she poured out her soul before the Lord, vowing that if God would give her a son, she would dedicate him to the Lord all his days. Hannah's desire for what God desired came out in the form of a two-letter word: *if.* As Hannah prayed, she was fully aware that bearing children and becoming a mother may not have been God's desire for her. She essentially said, "*If* You are willing, Lord, *if* this desire of mine lines up with Your desire, may it be done" (cf. 1 Sam 1:11).

Such a desire was found in Ruth when she unapologetically severed all ties to her nation, her family and her religion. Ruth clung to her mother-in-law Naomi, vowing to remain with her until death (Ruth 1:16–17).

Such a desire was found in Esther as she listened to her cousin Mordecai explain how an edict had been issued for the execution of her people. As Queen of Persia, Esther could have concealed her true identity and allowed the devastation and destruction of her people to occur. However, her desire for what God desired compelled her to boldly respond, "I will go in to the king, which is not according to the law; and if I perish, I perish" (Esth 4:16).

A Student of the Word

What about you? What are your desires as a woman? I'm not talking about where you see yourself in the next five or ten years; I'm not talking about how you can finally start building that dream home you've always wanted or launching that business or ministry you've always talked about. When you hear what God says in His Word concerning you as a woman, how do you respond? When you hear God's commands and expectations of you as a single woman, wife, or mother, do you dismiss it as if it was written for another woman in another time and place? Are your desires shaped by the Word of God?

True womanhood is an inward heart attitude and disposition whereby a woman acknowledges God's Word as the final authority and shaping influence in her life, not her pastor, not her mother, and not even her husband. Women today are violating God's Word, doing things in the church God never intended for a woman to do. Their justification for it is that their pastor gave them the authority and their husband gave them the permission. A transformed woman of God does not use her pastor or her husband in order to function in a role contrary to God's will for her. A pastor's authority and a husband's permission are important and necessary roles granted by God to be used only within the boundary of Scripture. Neither have authority that supersedes God's Word.

When God's Word is truly the final authority in a woman's life, she assertively refuses to allow herself to be influenced by a view or a course of action that is contrary to that Word.

Think about it. The enemy who approached Eve and influenced her to disregard what God said is the same enemy who relentlessly tries daily to get into your head and alter your thinking. Not only has he studied mankind from the beginning of the creation, but he also knows your particular weaknesses. He knew just what to say and how to say it to get Eve to rebel from what God intended for her. How much more so does he know us? He knows what works on us, and he regularly employs it.

Notice in the chart below how the Bible describes Satan:

Satan is a liar	Satan is a counterfeit	Satan is a destroyer
"He was a murderer from the beginning, and does not stand in truth because there is no truth in him. Whenever he speaks a lie, he speaks from his own nature, for he is a liar and the father of lies." (Jn 8:44)	"No wonder, for even Satan disguises himself as an angel of light." (2 Cor 11:14)	"The thief comes only to steal and kill and destroy; I came that they may have life, and have it abundantly." (Jn 10:10)
Satan uses the same words he has always used: **Lies**	*Satan uses the same methods he has always used:* **Deceit**	*Satan pursues the same goal he has always pursued:* **Ruin**

Dear Sis

Satan's "M.O." has always been the complete overthrow of God's order, design, and plan. What God declares as off limits, Satan gets you to respond to his declaration with cynicism. What God has established and ordained to function a certain way, Satan gets you to dismiss and exchange for what you think is a better or "practical" way (Prov 16:25).

Are you aware that the Word of God is put on display by how you live your life? When you open your mouth, can others tell you are a student of the Word? By the way you dress, by your conversations, by how you care for your family and the organizations with which you involve yourself, is it obvious that you are a transformed woman?

Always remember that a woman who knows God's Word, delights in God's Word, obeys, proclaims, and protects God's Word, is a beautiful force to be reckoned with. A woman like that will make Satan think twice before he comes after her (Luke 22:31)!

What Are Your Thoughts?

1. What stood out to you or caused you to raise an eyebrow in this chapter?

2. What do you think God meant by the phrase "helper suitable"? How would you define "helper suitable" in today's modern culture? Compare/contrast the two. Are there any lessons to be learned from the two definitions? If so, explain.

3. With her husband next to her and the fact that God took walks in the Garden of Eden (Gen 3:8), think about how Eve could have handled the situation with the serpent differently. What are some things she could have done instead of disobeying the Word of God?

4. What are some possible reasons why Eve did not defer to her husband when questioned by the serpent?

5. Why do you think Eve made a decision to eat from the forbidden tree without first discussing the serpent's new information with her husband? The new information shared by the serpent was "you will not die and you will be like God," implying that God had questionable motives.

6. Eve lived in a perfect and unbroken environment. We live in an imperfect and broken environment. Clearly, Eve thought the tree could improve her life. How does our desire to solve problems or improve our life make us vulnerable to deception? What can we do to lessen the possibility of being deceived in these endeavors?

On a Personal Note
What characteristics do you see in Eve that you also see in yourself?

CHAPTER 2

EVE 2.0: A Rogue State of Mind
(Genesis 2:9, 16–22; 3:1–12, 22)

> An excellent wife is
> the crown of her husband,
> but she who shames him
> is as rottenness in his bones.
>
> ---
>
> Proverbs 12:4

"A bittersweet cocktail of wisdom and absurdity" was one of the comments made about a book written by Rachel Held Evans, titled *A Year of Biblical Womanhood: How a Liberated Woman Found Herself Sitting on Her Roof, Covering Her Head and Calling Her Husband "Master."* This *New York Times* bestseller caught my attention because of the words "Biblical Womanhood" prominently displayed in the title on the front cover.

In *A Year of Biblical Womanhood,* Evans explains how she became intrigued by the decisions of many of her friends to abandon their careers and assume traditional gender roles in the home. As a result, she decided to embark on a radical life experiment of her own and vowed to "follow as many of the Bible's teachings regarding women as possible"[1] in her day-to-day life. The book was a detailed account of that experiment.

---

[1] Rachel Held Evans, *A Year of Biblical Womanhood* (Nashville: Thomas Nelson, 2012), xxi.

I wish I could tell you I found the book to be refreshing and inspiring, but that would simply not be true. What is true is that I felt it was even more disturbing than I anticipated. What was incredibly difficult about reading *A Year of Biblical Womanhood* was how the Bible at certain points was grossly distorted. While it had some humorous parts, there is absolutely nothing funny about undermining and twisting God's Word.

For example, Evans, who described herself as a follower of Jesus, flippantly called into question the holy, infallible, and inspired Word of God when she wondered:

> Could an ancient collection of sacred texts spanning multiple genres and assembled over thousands of years in cultures very different from our own, really offer a single cohesive formula for how to be a woman? And do all the women of Scripture fit into this same mold? Must I?[2]

In describing faith, she stated:

> Faith isn't about having everything figured out ahead of time; faith is about following the quiet voice of God without having everything figured out ahead of time. I didn't wait for certainty when I married Dan, I didn't wait for certainty when I wrote my first book, I didn't wait for certainty when I decided to follow Jesus—or when I started this project. I just listened to my heart and let love pull me through the unknown.[3]

Evans's experiment consisted of numerous manifestations of bizarre behavior, such as placing a scarf or hoodie on her head right before she prayed and addressing her husband as "Master." (She even stood along the

---

[2] Ibid., xx.
[3] Ibid., 188.

side of a busy Tennessee highway holding a "Dan is Awesome" sign.) Shockingly, she also slept on her front lawn during menstruation so as not to make her house "unclean" and sat on the roof of her house whenever she engaged in gossip and other kinds of slander.

Heard enough? It gets even better. Along with learning to cook, bake, and knit, Evans's experiment included renting an interactive, computerized doll that was programmed to simulate the twenty-four-hour demands of an infant, in order to cultivate her motherly instincts.

Visits to a monastery, an Amish schoolhouse and a sprawling pig farm in Bolivia, rounded out the whirlwind, yearlong experiment Evans defined as "biblical womanhood." Unbelievable, and as I said earlier, very disturbing!

One thing is for certain, the author went to great lengths to ridicule, mock, and poke fun at God's design and purpose for women. This is one reason why the instruction to women in Titus 2 is so critical. God's expectation is that we function and live in a certain way so that the Word of God will not be maligned, blasphemed, cheapened, or dishonored (Titus 2:5). The Apostle Peter put it this way:

> Keep your behavior excellent among the Gentiles, so that in the thing in which they slander you as evildoers, they may because of your good deeds, as they observe them, glorify God in the day of visitation. (1 Pet 2:12)

Biblical womanhood is not attempting to live out misunderstood and misinterpreted Scripture passages, as tragically portrayed in Evans's book. Nor is it a set of rules and commands that make you appear weird, out of touch with reality, and foolish.

And yet, sadly, the most devastating outcome of the book is the number of women who have or will read it. How tragic that countless women will be influenced to act, think, and adopt a view of life and of God that is so contrary to His Word.

Rachel Held Evans was not the first nor will she be the last person to mislead women into error and sin. As Solomon rightly said, "There is nothing new under the sun" (Eccl 1:9).

It is no surprise that the first person to distort the Word of God and mislead a woman was Satan. He influenced Eve in four key areas that inevitably resulted in rebellious behavior:

- Satan influenced Eve in the way she thought about God.
- Satan influenced Eve in the way she thought about God's command.
- Satan influenced Eve in the way she thought about the consequences of her actions.
- Satan influenced Eve in the way she related to her husband.

With no words spoken, as she "gave also to her husband with her," apparently Eve expected Adam to follow her lead. And he did! Eve sinned against her husband by not submitting to his leadership and thereby became a catalyst for him to disobey the Word of God, too. Essentially, Eve supplied the cover for Adam to rebel against the direct command of God. The result: Eve (and Adam) failed God.

Rather than displaying the Word of God through obedience, Eve disregarded God's clear command, followed her own desires, and exchanged the truth for a lie. Eve believed the information she was given. Eve trusted the source of the information. Eve believed acting on the information would benefit her and Adam. She unknowingly exchanged reality for an illusion and was oblivious to what was actually taking place. This is the nature of deception.

You have probably heard the analogy before, that rat poison is ninety percent food and ten percent poison. Although most of what the rat eats is actual food, it is the ten percent of poison that kills it. It's been said that falsehood and deception are not the same thing, that falsehood is ninety percent lie and ten percent truth, while deception is ninety percent truth and ten percent lie. Think about it. Ninety percent of what the serpent said to Eve was actually true (Gen 3:5, 22). However, the first five words of his comments—the ten percent, the bold-faced lie—were ignored by Eve, resulting in her being deceived.

Whatever thoughts and feelings Eve had about being like God and knowing good and evil were immediately met with the cruel, harsh reality of irrevocable bondage and the unimaginable loss associated with being separated from God.

Hook, Line, and Sinker

When Satan approached Eve in the garden, it was for the sole purpose of misleading her: "Has God indeed said, 'You shall not eat from any tree of the garden?'" (Gen 3:1). With one question, Satan managed to distort what God had said and cast doubt in Eve's mind about God's character.

The serpent's statements set the stage for Eve's own desires to move to front and center. His deceptive lure opened her mind up to the possibility of an alternative way of living, a way of living that gave rise to thoughts of personal satisfaction and entitlement. A cascade of thoughts about the Garden, about God's Word and, more significantly, about God's character may have flooded Eve's mind as she demonstrated no gratitude for the abundance God had placed her in. She wanted more. With the consequence of eating from the tree removed from the equation by the serpent ("You surely shall not die") and the prospect of personal benefits gained ("You will be like God, knowing good and evil"), there was nothing left to do but to partake.

Back in the day, the expression was "hook, line, and sinker." It refers to a person who acts upon information given them without question, hesitation, doubt, or reservation. In the world of fishing, a hook, line, and sinker are tools used to trick fish into biting the bait (worm), not knowing that a hook and line leading to their demise was underneath.

However, Eve was not deceived by a worm dangling from a fishing hook, and neither are we. The lust of the flesh, the lust of the eyes, and the boastful pride of life (1 John 2:16) are the bait Satan uses again and again. Yielding to it guarantees you will lose, you will fail, and ultimately, you will sin, which is precisely his goal. He wanted Adam and Eve to rebel against God, and that's exactly what he got.

Notice in the charts below the stark differences between what God said to Adam and what the serpent said to Eve.

To Adam, *God* said:

"From *any* tree of the garden you may eat *freely*" (Gen 2:16, emphasis added).	• God spoke authoritatively. • God emphasized the abundance and plentifulness ("any") to which Adam and Eve had access. • God's gracious generosity was on full display. • God encouraged open, independent, unlimited access to the fruit of the trees ("freely").
"But from the tree of the knowledge of good and evil you shall not eat, for in the day that you eat from it you shall *surely* die" (Gen 2:17, emphasis added).	• God specified only one tree that was off limits. • God clearly stated the command regarding the one tree and the consequence of violating the command.

To Eve, the *Serpent* said:

"'Indeed, has God said …?'" (Gen 3:1).	- Satan spoke with feigned ignorance. - Satan approached Eve with a contemptuous attitude. In today's vernacular, it might sound something like, "Did God just throw a command at you?"
"'… you shall not eat from any tree of the garden?'" (Gen 3:1)	- Satan distorted God's Word by emphasizing restriction rather than abundance. God had said, "From *any* tree of the garden you *may* eat *freely*."
"'You surely shall not die!'" (Gen 3:4)	- Satan outright lied to Eve. He said just the opposite of what God commanded and mocked God in the process.

Eve fell perfectly into Satan's evil plot when she responded to his deceptive inquiry. In an instant, she was at the point of no return:

> The woman said to the serpent, "From the fruit of the trees of the garden we may eat; but from the fruit of the tree which is in the middle of the garden, God has said, 'You shall not eat from it or touch it, or you will die.'" (Gen 3:2)

Notice how carelessly Eve herself handled, or rather mishandled, the Word of God:

- Eve left out God's bountiful provision and unlimited access (*any* and *freely*) in her statement.
- Eve referred to the forbidden tree, not by the title God gave it (the knowledge of good and evil), but rather "the tree in the middle of the garden."
- Eve ignored the other tree that was also in the middle of the garden, the tree of life (Gen 2:9).
- Eve added her own prohibition and attributed it to God (*"or touch it"*).
- Eve lessened the severity of judgment by stating, "You will die," rather than what God actually said, "You shall *surely* die."

Once Satan succeeded in misleading Eve in how she thought about what God said, autonomy and self-fulfillment became the focus. Eve acted according to what made her feel good about herself and her future and what made sense in her skewed thinking. As Genesis 3:6 points out, "When the woman saw that the tree was good for food and that it was a delight to the eyes and that the tree was desirable to make one wise, she took from its fruit and ate."

Your Mind Is Sought-After Territory

Have you ever thought about the strategy Satan employed in getting Eve and Adam to sin?

Eve was perfect and living in a perfect environment, yet Satan knew one thing about her. He knew that if he could gain control of her mind, her mind would do the work for him. If he could influence her thoughts, then he could direct her steps. Her reasoning would inevitably take her where he wanted her to go. This is one critical reason why the Word of God urges believers to:

- be careful how we walk (Eph 5:15)
- understand what the will of the Lord is (Eph 5:17)
- let the words of Christ dwell in us richly (Col 3:16)
- be transformed by the renewing of our minds (Rom 12:2)

Satan is crafty in his actions toward people. His craftiness is evident in that he uses very little effort to accomplish his goal. He did not escort Eve to the forbidden tree. He did not suggest that she eat from the tree or offer her its fruit. He simply manipulated her thinking through one question: "Did God really say?" He was easily able to lead her away from the truth once her careless handling of the Word of God became apparent to him (Gen 3:3).

Think about your most valuable asset. It may be your house or your car, or perhaps your 401k retirement plan. But to the enemy, your mind is the most valuable asset. It is important you are aware of and understand the high premium he has placed on your mind. He considers it prime real estate, and he is vying for control, or at least influence, over it continually. Desires, disappointments and difficulties of life are some of the entry points the devil uses to gain access to your mind and influence your thinking.

Satan is an expert at getting you to feel comfortable with questioning God's motives. He is an expert at getting you to think that your plans are just as good as God's and should be pursued. He's also an expert at getting you to feel you have the right to decide what is best for you. Satan specializes in getting you to take a chance on following your own ideas rather than following God's Word. He loves it when you tell yourself things like, *I've got this* or *What do I have to lose?*

Remember Sarah and Abraham? God promised to give them a son (Gen 15:4). Sarah most likely thought she would conceive in the next week or two and have a baby boy nine months later. But that didn't happen. Twenty-five years would go by before Sarah and Abraham would have Isaac, the promised son. I can imagine Sarah, when she devised a plan to help God fulfill His promise, thinking *What do I have to lose? I am well beyond childbearing years,* or *I am acting within my legal right and custom to have a child through my maidservant, Hagar.*

Your Mind is a Constant Battlefield

Because Satan is fixated on your mind, understand that it is being assaulted regularly. Things you see. Things you hear. How you feel at any given time. Situations and circumstances that occur in your life. All of these trigger thoughts. The music you listen to and what you watch on TV or at the movies generate thoughts that the enemy can use to distract you from God's plan for your life. As a follower of Christ, you are on active duty all the time, especially when it comes to your mind.

A few years ago, my two sons enlisted in the National Guard and are still serving. Once a month, they are required to report for training. They know that at any time, if necessary, they can be called up on active duty. They could be required to serve in Afghanistan, Syria, or some other battleground, and if deployed, they must serve the duration of the time needed before they can return home.

Similarly, as a believer, you signed up and were deployed for active duty the moment Christ saved you. You will remain in active duty until God calls you home to be with Him. There is no furlough. You are never off duty. Even when you're not thinking about anything, your mind is a target of the enemy, and he won't miss the opportunity to assault it. This is one reason we are reminded by the Apostle Peter that our enemy prowls around, seeking someone to devour (2 Pet 5:8).

Your Mind Can Be Influenced by the Enemy

Satan can only influence your mind if you allow him. While as a believer you can never be possessed by Satan or his demons, he can influence you as he did with Eve. He knows you are sealed in your faith. He knows you were purchased by the blood of the Lord Jesus and your eternal destiny is secure. That is unchanging. There is nothing he can do about your eternal destiny. But he can influence you to be ineffective.

Satan can use the sin of despair or discontentment to lead you to doubt God's love for you. He uses the discouragements of life to lead you to question God's faithfulness and goodness towards you. He can weaken your testimony by the choices you make or the things in the world with which you involve yourself. There is no doubt, he can influence your mind.

When you choose to engage in social media and neglect the study of God's Word and prayer, you are allowing the enemy access to your mind. When you are more faithful in attending a women's book club gathering than attending and participating in Sunday worship, you are allowing the enemy access to your mind.

When you choose to involve your children in numerous sporting events that will take them and you away from Sunday worship, you are giving the enemy an opportunity to affect your mind.

When your closest relationships are with people who do not love the Lord or have not prioritized His Word in their life, you are allowing the enemy access to your mind. In fact, anytime your agenda or desires do not line up with God's will, you are giving Satan an inroad to influence your thinking for his evil purposes.

Your Mind Matters to God

God is concerned about what goes on in your mind and holds you accountable for your every thought (1 Cor 4:5; Matt 12:36–37; 25:31–36; Mark 4:22; Luke 12:2–3). In contrast to what Satan wants, here are eight principles God wants you to operate by:

1. **Have a sound mind:** "For God has not given us a spirit of fear, but of power and love and a sound mind" (2 Tim 1:7).

2. **Be mentally at peace:** "The steadfast of mind You will keep in perfect peace, because he trusts in You" (Isa 26:3).

3. **Love Him with your mind:** "You shall love the Lord Your God with all your heart, and with all your soul, and with all your mind" (Matt 22:37).

4. **Renew your mind:** "And do not be conformed to this world, but be transformed by the renewing of your mind, so that you may prove what the will of God is, that which is good and acceptable and perfect" (Rom 12:2).

5. **Engage your mind in His Word:** "For these were more noble-minded than those in Thessalonica, for they received the word with great eagerness, examining the Scriptures daily to see whether these things were so" (Acts 17:11).

6. **Prepare your mind for action:** "Therefore, prepare your minds for action, keep sober in spirit, fix your hope completely on the grace to be brought to you at the revelation of Jesus Christ" (1 Pet 1:13).

7. **Guard your mind:** "Watch over your heart with all diligence, for from it flow the springs of life" (Prov 4:23).

8. **Set your mind on Him:** "Set your mind on the things above, not on the things that are on earth" (Col 3:2).

In order for these eight principles to become reality, you have to commit to knowing, meditating and memorizing the Word of God.

Think about your favorite meal or dessert. When you have it, you are not rushing to swallow it down and devour it! No, you want to savor it. The aroma, the flavor, and the texture ignite your taste buds as you enjoy each wonderful bite. The more you eat, the more you want.

The same should be true of the Word of God for you. Savor the Word of God as you take it in. Reading it should never be viewed as a chore to complete so you can get on with your day.

Early on in our marriage, Roger encouraged me to choose a book of the Bible and read through it several times for an entire month. As I did this, I found myself becoming more and more familiar with the people, culture and customs, key words, and events within that month's reading. I also found myself being able to recall where certain verses were located. I started to use this same method in memorization. Reading a verse or passage of Scripture again and again throughout the course of a month makes committing it to memory so much easier.

Another method of memorizing and meditating on the Word of God is by working with a prayer partner. If you have a prayer partner, the two of you could also memorize Scripture together. What a way to "savor" the Word of God.

Be encouraged by what David, Job, the prophet Jeremiah, and the Apostle Paul had to say about savoring the Word of God:

> How sweet are your words to my taste, sweeter than honey to my mouth! (Ps 119:103)

> I have treasured the words of His mouth more than my necessary food. (Job 23:12b)

> Your Words were found and I ate them, and Your Words became for me a joy and the delight of my heart; for I have been called by Your name, O Lord God of hosts. (Jer 15:16)

> Whatsoever things are true, whatsoever things are right, whatsoever things are lovely, whatsoever things are honorable, whatsoever things are pure, if there be any excellencies, if there be anything worthy of praise, think on these things. (Phil 4:8)

Committing to savoring the Word makes it increasingly difficult for our enemy to influence our mind to think and act in ways contrary to God's Word.

Dear Sis

From the moment Eve opened her mouth and began to speak, she was clearly an easy target for deception, and Satan pounced on the opportunity (1 Pet 5:8). She then proved the disastrous effects of giving in to her feelings instead of sticking to the facts. By her own admission, Eve knew the facts. She knew she was not to eat from the tree of the knowledge of good and evil. That was a fact. Even her added prohibition, "or touch it" (Gen 3:3), should have kept her far from the tree. It did not! It could not! Only when we yield to the Spirit of God and surrender our will to His can obedience to His Word take place.

What felt right to Eve was actually wholesale rebellion against God and rebellion against the very purpose for which she was created (Gen 2:18). Satan knew exactly what God said. However, what Eve should have realized was that nothing good was going to come out of a discussion about a tree that God had already said was off limits.

What Are Your Thoughts?

1. What stood out to you or caused you to raise an eyebrow in this chapter?

2. Why do you think Satan tries to influence the way we think about God?

3. Why are our feelings as women such a powerful tool for Satan?

4. What role does a woman's "intuition" play in influencing her feelings and behavior?

5. Do you see Eve in any of the following ways? If so, explain.

- A grateful person
- A planner
- A thinker
- Ambitious
- A team player
- An asset or a liability

6. When you think about the enemy being fixated on gaining control of your mind, how should you guard your mind?

On a Personal Note

Read Philippians 4:8 over the next several days and commit the verse to memory.

CHAPTER 3

Delilah: A Rogue Relationship

(Judges 13, 14, 15, 16)

> But for the cowardly and unbelieving
> and abominable and murderers
> and immoral persons and sorcerers
> and idolaters and all liars,
> their part will be in the lake that
> burns with fire and brimstone,
> which is the second death.
>
> ―――――――――――――――――
>
> Revelation 21:8

"How can you say, 'I love you,' when your heart is not with me?" (Judg 16:15). Those words were spoken by a woman whose name means dainty or delicate one. However, if you know anything about Delilah, you know that "dainty and delicate" was far from the task she was bribed and motivated to do. She was offered eleven hundred pieces of silver by each of the five lords of the Philistines if she could get Samson to disclose the source of his strength.

Unfortunately for Samson, that kind of money for a woman back then would have been very hard to pass up. John MacArthur explained what the amount would be in today's dollars as follows: "Biblical scholars have noted that the average yearly wage for a laborer was only ten silver shekels, making this offer five hundred fifty times that amount! If we compared that to wages of $50,000 today, the cash reward would have been almost $30 million."[15] Turning down an offer that would guarantee thirty million dollars today would be very hard to pass up. It was a fortune. Delilah would have been financially secure for several lifetimes.

Although this chapter is about Delilah, and our focus will remain on her, we have to talk for a moment about Samson. For there is no Delilah without Samson.

Who Was Samson?

At the prophecy of Samson's birth, his mother was told to "be careful not to drink wine or strong drink, nor eat any unclean thing. For behold, you shall conceive and give birth to a son and no razor shall come upon his head, for the boy shall be a Nazirite to God from the womb" (Judg 13:4–5). She was to live in that manner because Samson was chosen to be the one who would "begin to deliver Israel from the hands of the Philistines" (Judg 13:5). Samson was also to abstain from wine and strong drink. Lastly, he was not to cut his hair nor touch a dead body. This was to externally represent his commitment to living a holy life unto the Lord (Num 6:3–5).

From the moment of that prophecy, there was no doubt Samson was going to be a great man. God had set him apart. He was a Nazirite; the name means to separate or to be consecrated to God. However, being a great man was not going to mean that he would be devoid of error and flaws.

How One Lives Matters

Samson's flaws were numerous. Uncontrolled passions, sinful desires, fixation on the wrong kinds of women (Judg 14:1–3; 16:1, 4), blatant disregard for the commands of God (Judg 14:8–9), and severe anger issues (Judg 14:19; 15:4–15) all point to a man whose behavior was out of order.

---

[15] John MacArthur, *Twelve Unlikely Heroes* (Nashville: Thomas Nelson, 2012), 84.

Samson has been described as a biblical Paul Bunyan, a man larger than life, a Herculean man. However, his physical strength was no match for his overwhelming moral weakness. As Dr. Lockyer states in *All the Women of the Bible*, "Although able to rend a lion, he could not fight his lusts. He could break his bonds, but not his habits. He could conquer Philistines, but not his passions."[16]

Samson's weakness would ultimately prove to be stronger than his Herculean strength. How you live life matters especially to God. Samson did not live a holy life unto the Lord as his mother's vow required. In the end, the consequence of the lack of moral integrity and his flagrant sinfulness would lead to a horrific demise.

Although the Lord was with Samson in his interactions with the Philistines and at times the "Spirit of the Lord came upon him mightily" resulting in superhuman strength (Judg 14:6,19; 15:14), it was through the outcome of his relationship with Delilah that the Lord departed from him (Judg 16:20). For Samson, in all of his escapades and ungodly living, a time came when God's presence was no longer with him, and sadly, he experienced catastrophic suffering, pain, and death because of it.

Samson was captured by the Philistines with the help of Delilah. His eyes were gouged out, he was imprisoned, and he was forced to work as a grinder for the rest of his life (Judg 16:20–21). What's more, according to *The Expositor's Bible Commentary*, "Grinding at the mill was a woman's job, which added to Samson's humiliation. It is unclear whether he used a small hand mill or was forced to turn a large circular stone, a job normally given to donkeys."[17] Either way, it was demeaning for him.

And yet, in all the horror Samson suffered at the end of his life, God extended grace to him in one last act. Samson killed more Philistines at his

---

[16] Herbert Lockyer, *All the Women of the Bible* (Grand Rapids: Zondervan, 1973), 42.

[17] Kenneth L. Barker and John R. Kohlenberger III, *The Expositor's Bible Commentary: Abridged Edition* (Grand Rapids: Zondervan, 1994), 359.

death than in his life (Judg 16:30). During a time of celebration and sacrifice to their god Dagon, the Philistines brought him out of prison to entertain themselves. Positioned between two pillars,

> Samson called to the Lord and said, "O Lord God, please remember me and please strengthen me just this time, O God, that I may at once be avenged of the Philistines for my two eyes." (Judg 16:28)

God used Samson in his final hour to do what he was born to do. Samson delivered Israel from Philistine oppression. Years and years later, the author of Hebrews named Samson as one of the heroes of faith (Heb 11:32–34).

Samson's life was extraordinary, but not always in a good way. It was marked by extremely irrational, impulsive, and foolish behavior. His downfall began when he insisted on marrying a Philistine woman on the sole basis that she looked good to him. This was done against his father and mother's wishes (Judg 14:3); but, more importantly, it was done against God's law in which Israelites were not to intermarry with other nations. Then, a series of cascading tragic events occurred. First, Samson's wife was given to his companion (like a best man in a wedding) to marry without his knowledge (Judg 14:20). Samson responded by using three hundred foxes to burn up the Philistines' crops (Judg 15:5), which in turn led to the Philistines retaliating by burning Samson's wife and her father to death, resulting in Samson striking "them ruthlessly with a great slaughter" (Judg 15:8).

The very next thing we are told about Samson, beginning in chapter sixteen, is that he went to Gaza and had sexual relations with a prostitute (Judg 16:1), and then, "After this, it came about that he loved a woman in the valley of Sorek, whose name was Delilah" (Judg 16:1, 4). Notice that Samson had a one-night stand with one woman and fell in love with another woman.

The valley of Sorek was south of Zorah where Samson was born, and it extended near Jerusalem to the Mediterranean. No specific city or hometown is mentioned for Delilah. Some scholars say she could have been from Timnah, which is where Samson's wife lived when he first saw her.

Who Was Delilah?

Although Samson loved Delilah, interestingly, the Bible does not say that she loved him. How did they meet? How long had they been together when Samson realized he loved her? What was it about her that he loved? At least his former wife "looked good to Samson" (Judg 14:7). Have you ever wondered why she and Samson never married?

Delilah is an intriguing character. She is intriguing not because there was something extra special or unique about her. She is intriguing because she appears suddenly on the pages of Scripture and immediately the focus of a powerful and great man dramatically shifts to her. All attention is on Delilah, at least for a short while, though she does not rank anywhere near Samson's level of biblical significance. It is mind-boggling that she was able to keep Samson enthralled, though it was evident she was betraying him.

The basic information about her is revealed in ten words. She was a "woman in the valley of Sorek, whose name was Delilah" (Judg 16:4). In their Bible commentary, Kenneth Barker and John Kohlenberger further point out, "Delilah is never called a Philistine woman, but her proximity to the Philistine occupied area and her close contact with their leaders indicates that she probably was."[18]

We don't have information about her upbringing, her parents, or other family. No information about her background is mentioned. However, she is the only woman referenced by name in the Bible's account of Samson's life. His mother, his former wife, and even the prostitute he slept with in Gaza are all unnamed. In fact, Delilah's name is so intrinsically tied to his

---

[18] Ibid., 358.

that it is difficult to think of the story of Samson without also thinking of her.

Delilah was approached directly by the highest-ranking men in Philistia (Judg 16:5). The lords, or rulers, of Philistia would be similar to government officials in modern times. In those days and culture, that a group of high-ranking officials would enlist the help of a woman to take down of a mighty man was a huge red flag. Something was very wrong with that scenario, and everybody involved knew it. Men hardly spoke to women in that day, much less enlist their help in subduing and overpowering their enemy.

Lastly, Delilah is intriguing because, once she completed her task, she was neither seen nor heard of again on the pages of Scripture. What happened to her? Did she remain in town once she received her fortune? Was she among the three thousand who lost their lives when "the house fell on the lords and all the people who were in it" (Judg 16:30)? Was she remorseful after seeing Samson in shackles with his eyes gouged out, knowing she willingly took part in his defeat? The Bible does not tell us. However, Delilah remains a symbol of all that was damning and disastrous in Samson's life.

Delilah's Dealings

The kind of woman Delilah was played a huge role in her success at getting Samson to disclose the source of his strength. Her character and reputation are synonymous with ruin and all things deadly. She and women like her represent the worse in womanhood. Notice with me the numerous character flaws that marked Delilah's life:

- negative reputation
- driven by greed
- deceitful
- disloyal
- indifferent

- evil to the core
- heartless
- cunning and sly

Let's look at these character flaws a little more closely.

It is not hard to imagine that Deliliah's *negative reputation* preceded her. Apparently, she was known in the valley of Sorek and caught the attention of the rulers of Philistia. They seemed to know her and had no problem approaching her (Judg 16:5).

They concluded that the best person to spearhead their dirty work was not amongst themselves but a woman whose name meant "dainty." Clearly, there was something about Delilah that made her a good match for the task.

The Philistine lords focused on one woman to get the job done. They had no intentions of looking for another. The astronomical amount of money offered may indicate that perhaps she was not one to run the risk of losing. Just to put things in perspective, when Judas betrayed Jesus, it was for thirty pieces of silver, a considerably less amount than what Delilah was offered.

Delilah was *driven by greed*, which is not surprising. Eleven hundred pieces of silver was very hard to come by in that day, just as thirty million dollars is hard to come by in ours. When that kind of money is within a person's reach, greed will do whatever is necessary. Delilah was clearly motivated to do what was necessary!

Delilah was *deceitful* and apparently had no problem betraying Samson's love. Upon being approached by the Philistine lords, she apparently had no shocked look on her face and no hesitancy in her spirit. She asked no questions of the men. She did no second-guessing as to how the whole process would work. As if she'd been waiting for just such an opportunity of a lifetime, she listened to the Philistines. She took them at their word. She was all too ready and immediately went to work on Samson. Money is a huge motivator!

Delilah was *disloyal* and *indifferent*. While of course she never told Samson about being approached by the lords of Philistia and offered money to betray him, her cold and calculating interactions with him made it clear that she had no affection for him as she repeatedly pressed him to reveal the source of his strength. When he kept lying, she went so far as to equate his secrecy with unfaithfulness, putting him on a guilt trip (Judg 16:15).

It would seem Samson and Delilah were made for each other. He, too, was disloyal and indifferent to Delilah and to God. He kept feeding his sexual appetite in spite of obvious betrayal. He claimed to love her, yet did not relate to her as a person.

Samson broke every religious vow and lived a life of wanton pleasure. He was impulsive and gratified his desires at leisure. He knew what God expected of him yet broke trust early on in his life. God gave him supernatural strength to tear a lion in half, yet he revisited and touched the dead carcass filled with honey from a beehive. He ate the honey and even gave some to his parents, never telling them from where the honey had come (Judg 14:8–9; Num 6:1–6). This was a direct violation of his vow.

The flaws in Samson's character are evidence that he was the type of person who would abandon holiness and spiritual cleanliness for personal pleasure.

Healthy relationships are built on mutual trust, respect, and protection. Devoid of these qualities, the relationship becomes characterized by disloyalty and indifference. It was clear from the beginning that Samson and Delilah were both only in the relationship for what they could get out of it.

Delilah was *evil to the core, heartless, cunning,* and *sly*. Delilah was not bothered one iota that she was consciously choosing to do the wrong thing. She consciously chose to carry out an evil deed. She may not have known the full extent of what the rulers of Philistia were going to do to Samson once they captured him, but she knew that what she was doing was wrong.

This is the calling card of an unhinged woman: she willingly chooses to do wrong even if others are hurt. She has no reset button that would cause her to reevaluate and abort her wicked actions. Her decisions are based on self-gratification. If there is something pleasing to gain, the unhinged woman will go for it every time.

Some say money isn't everything, but I can imagine Delilah laughing out loud at that. To her, money was absolutely everything. When Samson lied to her three times, rather than give up, she persisted.

When all else fails, a woman like Delilah will employ the last and most lethal weapon in her arsenal: pestering, better known as nagging. This is what the Proverbs 21 woman is best known for because verse 9 says, "It is better to live in a corner of a roof than in a house shared with a contentious woman," and verse 19 says, "It is better to live in a desert land than with a contentious and vexing woman."

Solomon had a lot to say about a nagging woman. He would know! He had seven hundred wives and three hundred concubines to care for in his lifetime (1 Kgs 11:1–3). In addition to those verses in Proverbs 21, he says, "A constant dripping on a day of steady rain and a contentious woman are alike" (Prov 27:15; see also Prov 19:13).

Potiphar's Wife (Gen 39:1–23)

Delilah was not the only unhinged woman that got a man captured and imprisoned. Potiphar's wife preceded her. She also got a man captured and imprisoned. Joseph was that man! But Joseph was innocent. It's one thing to continually disobey God's commands, live in a context of lies and deception, and foolishly ignore warning signs, resulting in bondage and imprisonment as Samson did. It's a totally different thing to be imprisoned because you vehemently rejected a woman's sexual advances, who then lied by accusing you of a crime you did not commit. This is what happened to Joseph.

Joseph was the first-born son of Rachel, the woman Jacob truly loved (Gen 29:18–20). He was first in Jacob's heart and loved more than all his brothers (Gen 37:4). This, for obvious reasons, was the cause of intense animosity and hatred towards him.

His bad report about his brothers to their father disclosing the meaning of a couple of dreams that depicted him to be superior to his family turned an already tense situation into an unbearable one for Joseph's brothers. No longer wanting to tolerate the sight of him, jealous and angry enough to kill him, his brothers sold him into Egyptian slavery (Gen 37:1–28).

Joseph was taken to Egypt where Potiphar, Pharoah's officer and the captain of the royal bodyguard, bought him (Gen 39:1–2). In spite of the adversity in his life, Joseph was a faithful, godly man. Because the Lord was with him, he prospered as a slave and was successful in his master's household (Gen 39:2–3). However, unbeknownst to him, he was being watched. He was being observed. He was no doubt the subject of numerous romantic fantasies carried out in the mind of Potiphar's wife. The Bible says he was "handsome in form and appearance" (Gen 39:6) and she had definitely taken notice.

Joseph may have known that he was good-looking, but he had no way of knowing he would attract the attention of his master's wife. He also had no way of knowing that she would come at him hard and heavy, relentlessly tempting him day after day. It seems like she even tried to make it easier for him to sin by coaxing him to simply be with her, to keep her company (Gen 39:10).

The Bible gives us less information about Potiphar's wife than it does about Delilah. Potiphar's wife holds the dishonor of being the first unhinged woman mentioned in Scripture. In his sketch of Potiphar's wife, H. V. Morton stated that "she occupies a prominent place as the first sensualist in the gallery of Scriptural women."[19]

The Bible does not tell us anything about Potiphar's wife's upbringing or family connections. She had money because she was married to a wealthy Egyptian, but apparently, she had no children. With no real purpose defined

---

[19] H.V. Morton, quoted in Lockyer, *All the Women of the Bible*, 176.

in Scripture, I think it is safe to say that Potiphar's wife was a rich, bored, and idle woman, which makes for a diabolical combination.

While Potiphar's wife is one of the nameless women of the Bible, what she lacked in name identification she made up for in cruelty. Her entrance into the story of Joseph exposed her for the kind of woman she was. Her adulterous heart was in full bloom as she "looked with desire at Joseph and said, 'Lie with me'" (Gen 39:7).

Mrs. Potiphar was straightforward. She did not mince words, which may have been an indication that this was not her first rodeo. She was bold and most likely dressed to entice. She knew she had what any man would want. Why waste time with sweet talk and flattery? She got right to the point because she anticipated total and complete indulgence, not rejection.

Perhaps because she was the wife of one of Pharoah's prominent court officials, she felt she could have and take whatever she wanted when she wanted it. Perhaps she felt she did not have to play by the rules of fidelity and have only one man for one lifetime. Perhaps what she had in Potiphar had lost its appeal and had become boring, dull, or even repulsive. Joseph presented a new opportunity for real happiness and satisfaction. Perhaps she thought her looks would ignite Joseph's sexual passions as his did hers.

Whatever Potiphar's wife felt or thought, Scripture does not tell us. What we do know is clear by her actions, that she had long left "the companion of her youth" (Prov 2:17).

Joseph was a man of honesty and integrity, but, above all, he was a man of God. Although the law had not yet been given by God to His people, Joseph knew that taking another man's wife was wrong. So much so that Joseph not only refused the aggressive advances of Potiphar's wife but also tried to reason with her. He explained to her how he had been put in charge of all that belonged to Potiphar to the point that Potiphar had not a care or concern about any of his affairs except "the food which he ate" (Gen 39:6). He explained that Potiphar had withheld nothing from him except her (Gen 39:9).

He then asked a rhetorical question that should have set her attention front and center on God: "How then could I do this great evil and sin against God?" Perhaps he had hoped she would leave him alone.

Joseph loved God. He acknowledged God in his life. Would Potiphar's wife finally see him for the godly man he was? Would she back off and realize whatever dreams she had been having about their being together were never going to happen? No! Profoundly no! Apparently, all that talk and careful explanation went in one ear and out the other. It would seem Mrs. Potiphar heard not one word Joseph had said to her. And worse, she didn't care.

Potiphar's wife didn't care about the position Joseph had acquired. She didn't care that he had been given full governing control over all that her husband owned. She didn't care about the trust he had gained from her husband. She didn't care about his integrity. She didn't care about his reputation. She didn't care about Joseph, and she certainly didn't care about the God he served. Potiphar's wife dug in her heels even more and continued coming at him for one thing and for one thing only.

Let's continue reading:

> It came about as she spoke to Joseph day after day, that he did not listen to her to lie beside her or be with her. Now it happened one day that he went into the house to do his work, and none of the men of the household was there inside. (Gen 39:10–11)

None of the men were in the house? How much would you bet this whole scene was arranged? How much would you bet that Mrs. Potiphar had arranged for every one of the men of the household to be somewhere else, doing something else at the exact moment Joseph would be entering the house? Remember, she had been watching him for a while. She knew his schedule. She knew the precise time he would be there. How coincidental is it that all of the men would be gone, all at the same time?

Also, keep in mind that Joseph had already told Potiphar's wife, "My master does not concern himself with anything in the house" (Gen 39:8). Potiphar was certainly not around, and he didn't have to be. He had Joseph taking care of the matters of the house, so it was highly unlikely for him to pop in unexpectedly. Joseph had full authority over not only what took place in the house but the men (other slaves) who worked there, as well. Only one other person could order a whole group of slaves to be engaged elsewhere, and that person was Mrs. Potiphar!

Because Joseph did not succumb to her sexual advances, she resorted to a much more deviant approach. She grabbed him by his garment while inviting him to lie with her (Genesis 39:12).

How many times do you think she played that scene out in her mind? How many times had she thought about how things were going to go down that day? Perhaps she imagined, *Once I grab him and pull him in close, he will want me.* But, as I said earlier, she did not know Joseph, and she certainly did not know the God Joseph loved and served, because he responded by fleeing from her, leaving his garment in her hand (Gen 39:12).

Much has already been written, preached, and illustrated about Joseph and how he fled immorality. All of it may be great and wonderful and true. He absolutely did the right thing. But this is where the story hits us hard, and we find ourselves getting more and more angry as the events unfold:

> When she saw that he had left his garment in her hand and had fled outside, she called to the men of her household and said to them, "See, he has brought in a Hebrew to us to make sport of us; he came in to me to lie with me and I screamed. It came about when he heard that I raised my voice and screamed that he left his garment beside me and fled and went outside." So she left his garment beside her until his master came home. (Gen 39:13–16)

If you were an observer of this, wouldn't you find it strange that there was no evidence or mention of her physically trying to fight Joseph off? Wouldn't you find it strange that no other women were brought into the house to help comfort the traumatized wife who had just supposedly been attacked? Neither is there any mention of any of the men offering her sympathy. There seemed to be no rush or urgency on her part to notify her husband to return home to console her. After all, she had accused Joseph of attempted rape!

Furthermore, how is it that the men heard her when she called to them but did not hear her supposedly scream before she called for them? That's very odd. And wouldn't it seem strange that she "left his garment beside her until his master came home" (Gen 39:16)? What woman would want to remain next to the garment of the man who just tried to sexually assault you? Her story (lie) makes no sense.

I can imagine the men were oh too familiar with the morally corrupt wife and her evil ways. I can imagine the men thinking, *Here we go again!* The Bible doesn't say what they felt, let alone what their facial expressions were, but I can imagine they were frustrated, annoyed, and downright angry.

When Potiphar later came home, his wife continued her big lie:

> Then she spoke to him with these words, "The Hebrew slave whom you brought to us, came in to me to make sport of me; and it happened as I raised my voice and screamed, that he left his garment beside me and fled outside." So Joseph's master took him and put him into the jail, the place where the king's prisoners were confined; and he was there in the jail. (Gen 39:17–18, 20)

This is not what we want to read. We want to read about justice being done and Mrs. Potiphar getting exactly what was coming to her. We want to read about an apology being offered and Joseph's reputation remaining intact. Yet, the story keeps going from bad to worse, so much so that this innocent man of God paid a high price for doing the right thing.

Let me say again, this is not what we expect. This is not what we expect to happen to Joseph or anyone else who does the right thing. This is not what we expect or want to happen to us when we do what is right. We expect bad things to happen when we do bad things, and we expect good things and greater things to happen when we do right things.

Yet, God never promised bad for bad and good for good every single time. If He had, there would be no need for the Book of Job in the Bible. God never promised Joseph, you or me that life would be easy and free from hurt, pain, lies, accusations, loss, and ongoing difficult circumstances.

We tend to think that when everything in our life is going well and free of trouble, God is showering His blessings on us. We think He is pleased with us and causing our life to prosper. That may be true! However, we also tend to think that trials and hardships are a sign of God's judgment, that when things are going wrong, God must be judging us. Yet sometimes we are going to suffer and experience very difficult circumstances even when we have acted righteously (1 Pet 2:19–20). Nevertheless, we can be encouraged even through our sufferings as we obey God's commands and trust His promises as stated in such passages as John 16:33; 1 Peter 4:12; and Hebrews 12:7. And as for Potiphar's wife and others like her, the Bible has very strong words of warning in the following passages: Revelation 22:15; Proverbs 19:9; and Proverbs 6:16–19, among others.

Dear Sis

Delilah became the epitome of the nagging wife—like the drip, drip, drip of a broken faucet. She tore into Samson relentlessly, like the fangs of a lion tearing into its prey.

This is classic manipulation 101. Manipulation is an attempt to control someone in order to get them to do what you want them to do. Delilah was a master manipulator. Notice, Samson did not give in for the sake of "real love." There was none. Nor did he give in because he felt bad about keeping secrets from Delilah. He gave in because she badgered him. And she probably didn't even break a sweat. With all of Samson's magnificent strength, he was apparently hopelessly weak with a woman like her.

Delilah was an unhinged woman. She was a woman given over to the lusts of her heart. "It came about when she pressed him daily with her words and urged him, that his soul was annoyed to death" (Judg 16:16). That means Delilah was so thorough in her tactics that Samson would rather be dead than endure her verbal assaults.

"The love of money is a root of all sorts of evil" (1 Tim 6:10), and Delilah was offered a boatload of it. Come hell or high water, she was going to get that money!

Also, regarding our brief study of Potiphar's wife, we are reminded of several truths:

- **Adultery, as with all sin, begins in the heart.** Long before Mrs. Potiphar's plan was put in motion, adultery had already taken place in her heart.
- **What is in the heart will manifest itself.** Mrs. Potiphar's adulterous heart led her to desire, fantasize about, and pursue a man who was not her husband.
- **What is in the heart dictates your actions.** Mrs. Potiphar saw a good-looking man, and without any reservation, she wanted him. Her adulterous heart caused her to be dissatisfied and discontented with her husband.
- **What is in the heart overtakes your conscience.** When Mrs. Potiphar was repeatedly rejected, she vindictively fabricated a story and falsely accused Joseph. She had no problem lying even though it could lead to a death sentence for him. That Potiphar "took him and put him into the jail" (Gen 39:20) when he could have had

Joseph put to death is an indication that Potiphar may have been suspect of his wife's allegations (Matt 5:27–28; 15:19).

Mrs. Potiphar apparently had no remorse over her actions. She was heartless. Because the Bible makes no further mention of her, it would seem that Mrs. Potiphar got away with murder. No, she did not physically kill Joseph, but she certainly killed his reputation. She killed his spirit. She took away his freedom. She brought him to ruin.

But the Lord was with Joseph in spite of all the negative things that had happened and caused whatever he did to prosper (Gen 39:21, 23). God loved Joseph and was with him. Still, Joseph remained in prison for quite some time, all because of the lies of a vicious woman. Sometimes the things God allows to happen to us feel more like disdain than love. However, I think Joseph explained his situation best when, years later, he told his brothers, "You meant evil against me, but God meant it for good" (Gen 50:20).

What Are Your Thoughts?
1. What stood out to you or caused you to raise an eyebrow in this chapter?

2. How are Delilah and Mrs. Potiphar alike? How are they different?

3. In today's modern world, how might Delilah be characterized?
   - Smart
   - Daring
   - Courageous
   - Desperate
   - Man-hater
   - Other

4. The Bible does not indicate that Delilah was a woman of God. However, how might a Christian woman rationalize living with a

man who could significantly improve her financial standing? Now imagine she was your girlfriend; how would you speak the truth to her in love?

5. Is there anything a woman can do to keep from becoming the target of a man's sexual advances? If so, explain.

6. If you are a single female, what can you learn from how Joseph responded to sexual aggression and pursuit?

On a Personal Note

For single women wanting to get married, does the amount of money a man makes weigh heavier than his commitment to Christ and obedience to His Word? Why or why not?

CHAPTER 4

The Adulterous Wife: A Rogue Encounter

(Proverbs 5:3–5; 6:25–26, 32; 7:1–27; 30:20)

> Do not desire her beauty in your heart,
> nor let her catch you with her eyelids.
> For on the account of a harlot one is
> reduced to a loaf of bread and an
> adulteress hunts for the precious life.
>
> Proverbs 6:25–26

How many times have you heard about someone's life coming to ruin due to sexual indiscretions? How many times have you heard about a marriage destroyed and a reputation tarnished because of an inappropriate relationship? How many times have you heard about a high-profile figure or celebrity being involved in some sort of sex scandal? Too many times! It is sad but true.

Unfortunately, as we've seen so far with Samson, even the Bible, from the Old to the New Testament, contains numerous stories of people involved in sexual sin. Yet, no other book of the Bible has as many references and warnings against sexually loose women than the Book of Proverbs, with chapter 7 describing one of the more graphic stories.

Read Proverbs 7

Proverbs 7 begins with a loving father exhorting his son not only to listen to his commandments but to write them on the tablet of his heart, view them as the apple of his eye, and respect them as he would an intimate friend.

By observing the actions of a foolish young man, the father sternly warns his son about the devastating and destructive nature of getting involved with "the adulteress, the foreigner who flatters with her words" (Prov 7:5). He carefully explains to his son who she is, what she does and how she goes about doing what she does. Her lips, her words, her walk, her character, her appearance, and her ways all reveal a woman who is "bitter as wormwood and sharp as a two-edged sword" (Prov 5:4). It is for certain that men (and women) should beware of her kind.

One of the defining characteristics of the young male character the father describes to his son is the lack of sense (Prov 7:7). Notice some of the more obvious ways in which he lacked sense:

- He was undisciplined and acted irresponsibly (vv. 8–9)
- He was out at a ridiculous hour (v. 9)
- He was open to whatever the evening brought about (vv. 8–9)
- He put himself in a position to be tempted (vv. 8–9)
- He was looking for a certain kind of woman (v. 10)

While most likely he had planned to return home at some point, sadly the young man was oblivious to the fact that participating "in the unfruitful deeds of darkness" would eventually "cost him his life" (Ephesians 5:11; Proverbs 7:23).

I Have Done Nothing Wrong

An adulterous woman is, among other things, a dangerously unusual woman. Why? Because while women by our very nature are life givers, the adulteress is just the opposite. She is deadly with a one hundred percent success rate (Prov 2:18–19).

Part of what God created and endowed women to do was to give life. The first command God gave Adam and Eve in the Garden of Eden was to "be fruitful, multiply and fill the earth" (Gen 1:28). One of the reasons God said, "It is not good for the man to be alone" (Gen 2:18) was because Adam could not fulfill that command by himself. He needed a woman. He needed a helper suitable. He needed a life giver. God used Adam and Eve to create life, but He used Eve to give birth to that life. Besides subduing and ruling the earth alongside her husband, Eve was also given the responsibility of being a life giver. After all, her very name means "life," "life-giving," or "mother of all who have life."

Yet, in Proverbs 7, we find a woman who, rather than giving life, is viciously taking life away (Prov 7:26). So brash and unremorseful, the adulteress "eats and wipes her mouth and says, 'I have done no wrong'" (Prov 30:20). She is the kind of woman who knows exactly what she is doing. She knows exactly what she wants and how to present herself to get it. Even her conscience frees her up to keep at it, because it tells her there is nothing wrong with what she is doing. She is bold and precise in her methods. To make matters worse, "with her flattering lips she seduces" (v. 21). In other words, she is a very good talker. She knows what to say and how to say it. She is skilled in the art of persuasion.

As a married woman, the adulteress was supposed to be a "helper suitable" (Gen 2:18). She was to do her husband "good and not evil all the days of her life" (Prov 31:12). Instead, she does him wrong. She exploits him. She uses his business travel (Prov 7:18–20) to her own sinful advantage.

While the Bible has much to say about sexual sins, no more critical verse speaks to this topic more than what Paul told the church at Corinth in his first letter to them. The Corinthian church had a myriad of problems, from divisions among the people, to spiritual superiority issues, to lawsuits and the mishandling of the communion service. One of the most devastating problems was that a young man was having sex with his stepmother, and shockingly, the church was silent about it. Even the broader church was involved in temple prostitution. Although we are confronted with numerous things on a daily basis that can harm our physical body, none rise to the level of sexual sins against which Paul sternly admonished:

> Flee immorality. Every other sin that a man [*or woman*] commits is outside the body, but the immoral man [*or woman*] sins against his [*or her*] own body. (1 Cor 6:18, emphasis added)

What God created to be enjoyable, safe, and honorable in the context of marriage between one man and one woman becomes harsh, disastrous, shameful, unrelenting of pain and laced with ramifications that will linger long after the act is over.

This reminds me of a popular illustration that you've probably heard before. Fire in a fireplace is beautiful to look at and to experience. It is productive, warm, and inviting. But that same fire outside of a fireplace is devastating, destructive, and deadly. Just like an adulterous relationship.

Characteristics of an Adulteress

An adulteress has numerous identifying character traits, including but not limited to the following:

- inviting
- engaging
- destructive
- attractive
- aggressive
- desirable
- connected to death
- evil

- permanently reduces/lessens
- wounds
- distorts the marriage relationship
- unholy
- unrepentant

Notice what else the Bible says about the adulteress:

> For on account of a harlot one is reduced to a loaf of bread and an adulteress hunts for the precious life. (Prov 6:26)

> The one who commits adultery with a woman is lacking sense; he who would destroy himself does it. (Prov 6:32)

> Therefore God gave them over in the lusts of their hearts to impurity so that their bodies would be dishonored among them. (Rom 1:24)

Let's examine more closely just a few of the adulterous woman's traits.

The adulteress is a predator.

> And behold a woman comes to meet him. (Prov 7:10)

How did the adulteress know "in the twilight, in the evening, in the middle of the night, in the darkness" (v. 9) that a man was walking near her house? Why was she awake? How is it that she was prepared and ready to receive guests at that hour? Because she is a predator. She is aggressive. She is continually on the hunt.

Not wanting him to perhaps come to his senses and turn back, she did not wait for him to come to her door, when he took "the way to her house" (v. 8) but rather came out of her house to meet him. Like a hunter, the adulteress watches, observes and waits for the right moment to make her approach. She notices everything about her potential victim and uses it to her advantage. Clearly, the young man is not her first catch, nor is he her last. The encounter was an all too familiar scene, orchestrated by her to ensure a favorable outcome.

The adulteress has a single-minded focus.

Dressed as a harlot and cunning of heart. (Prov 10)

The adulteress captures the attention of men to arouse and hijack their sexual drive. Her attire does most of the work for her, especially given the fact that men are visually stimulated. It communicates that she not only has an insatiable desire for sex but that she is available and ready. To anyone who sees her, and certainly to the young man who is wandering on her street, there is no question of who she is and what she seeks.

With a bold, brash, and conquering attitude, the adulteress holds nothing back. She believes in being free to sexually express herself. Her attire along with a "cunning heart" have brought her much success in her trade, because "many are the victims she has cast down and numerous are all her slain" (Prov 7:26).

The adulteress is unruly.

Boisterous and rebellious. (Prov 11)

The adulteress is unstable, out of control to her very core and exactly what you would expect of a woman with wandering feet. She finds her place amongst heavy social activity because she's got it going on, but for all the wrong reasons. She's typically out and about with the pleasure seekers and the partygoers. In verse 12, the father describes her as first being "in the streets" then "in the squares" and then, if that doesn't make your head spin, she's also lurking by every corner. Think about that for a moment. She is lurking by *every* corner. So what exactly is the father's point here? This kind of woman can be found anywhere, not just in the red light district. This kind of woman can be found at your job, in your neighborhood, at the grocery store and, yes, even at church. Not even church is off limits to this kind of woman. She will plant herself right in a church if it means getting the "catch."

The more time she spends outside of her home, the greater opportunity it affords her to secure another conquest to satisfy her sexual appetite. She is both radical and riveting at the same time. Her lips drip honey, her speech is smoother than oil and her steps lay hold of Sheol (Prov 5:3–5).

Since this kind of woman is on the hunt, she's looking, watching, trying to make eye contact with men so she can wink, flirt and do whatever it takes to get their attention. Her eyes, like her attire, are another important component in catching her prey. As Solomon warns, "Do not desire her beauty in your heart, nor let her capture you with her eyelids" (Prov 6:25).

The adulteress is serious about what she does. She makes her presence known whether men are interested or not. All hours of the day and night, she stays busy mastering her craft. This is her pattern. This is her routine. This is her life.

The adulteress is brazen and unashamed.

> She seizes him and kisses him. (Prov 13)

The father continues to describe the adulteress's mode of operation. Dressed-to-kill, she immediately throws her arms around the young man's neck, pulls him close to her lips, and without hesitation, begins kissing him. While still interlocked in a kiss, she no doubt looks him squarely in the eye, a look that would settle any remaining reservations he may have, a look that says her body could be his, inviting him in and welcoming him to have her.

Does she even know the man's name, where he was the night before or where he is headed? Does she know anything about him? Is he also married? Does he have a family depending on him? None of that matters to her. All this wayward wife cares about is the fulfillment of her own sensual gratification, and for that, any man would do.

The adulteress is deceptive.

> I was due to offer peace offerings. (Prov 14)

Just as the enemy in the Garden of Eden influenced Eve down a path that ended in physical and spiritual ruin, the adulteress, by controlling the conversation, physically asserting herself and manipulating the emotions of her victims, guides men on a sexual path to ruin.

The adulteress makes herself appear to be religious by participating in a peace offering. Keep in mind that peace offerings were offered in the temple and a portion brought home to eat in a ceremonial supper. According to the law of peace offerings, the meat left over after the sacrifice was to be consumed before the end of the day (Lev 7:15). Knowing she would have meat left over from the sacrifice provides the perfect additional lure to help her get what she is after. She invites the young man into her house to join her for a meal, as she could not eat all the leftover meat alone.

She delivers a series of five statements designed to set the young man's mind at ease. She tells him his involvement with her is reasonable and beneficial and devoid of consequences. How familiar this sounds to what took place in the Garden of Eden.

Notice how she coerces him to accept her offer (vv. 14–20):

Statement	Today's Vernacular
"I was due to offer peace offerings. Today I have paid my vows." (v. 14)	*I am a woman of faith. Spirituality is important to me.*
"Therefore, I have come out to meet you, to seek your presence earnestly, and I have found you." (v. 15)	*I have been looking for a man like you.*
"I have spread my couch with coverings, with colored linens of Egypt. I have sprinkled my bed with myrrh, aloes and cinnamon." (v. 16)	*Your happiness means everything to me.*
"Come, let us drink our fill of love until morning, let us delight ourselves with caresses." (v. 18)	*We can have a good time tonight. I'll make it worth your while.*
"For the man is not at home. He has gone on a long journey, he has taken a bag of money with him, at full moon he will come home." (vv. 19–20)	*You are safe with me, and besides, no one will ever know.*

The adulteress is tantalizing.

With her many persuasions she entices him. (v. 21)

The adulteress knows how to stroke a man's ego. She not only knows what a man wants to hear, she knows how to say it. She has mastered the sultry tone of voice and how to work it. Is it any surprise that a woman who is predatory, brazen and unashamed, loud, wild, unruly and deceptive, and working with a single-minded focus would also be tantalizing? She planned out every detail of her deceptive, ruinous ways and left nothing to chance.

For the adulterous woman, her purpose and ultimate goal of obtaining "the precious life" (Prov 6:26) is always at the forefront of her mind. From her attire that caught his eye, to her flattering words and gestures that captured his heart, she covered all the sensual bases. And if those were to fail, she could rely on her kisses to serve as the initiation into the sexual encounter. Couched in an array of beauty, the proverbial arrow that pierces the young man's liver (verse 23) has already been released.

At this point, the young man is completely blinded with passion and unaware that what he thinks will bring him exhilarating pleasure is all an illusion. The adulterous woman's enticing offer has overtaken his emotions, her flattering words have interfered with his ability to reason, and her seductive embrace has clouded his vision to see the obvious. What a tragedy! What a waste!

Three emphatic and imperative statements close out this very sad story that a loving father is using to warn his son:

- Listen and pay attention to the words of my mouth (Prov 7:24).
- Do not let your heart turn aside to her ways (Prov 7:25).
- Do not stray into her paths (Prov 7:25).

It is interesting that these three imperatives are repeated numerous times throughout Proverbs, and in a broader sense, throughout the Bible when you realize that the story of the adulterous woman could be a representation of sin in general. Like the adulterous woman, sin is available everywhere and at all times of the day or night. It has been said, "You don't have to be looking for immorality, immorality is looking for you." The question becomes, are you going to be its next victim?

Remember, among the characteristics of an unhinged woman is that she does not ponder the path of life; her ways are unstable, and she does not know it. Why? Why does she not ponder the path of life? Why are her ways unstable? It is because of the choices she makes. It all starts with choices.

At some point in her life, the adulteress made the choice to "leave the companion of her youth and forget the covenant of her God" (Prov 2:17) in exchange for an adulterous lifestyle. But, how? How does a woman blow up her marriage, ruin her reputation, lose her family, and destroy relationships with the people who once loved her but now wonder about her and look at her side-eyed?

Choices Have Consequences

No woman wakes up one day and finds herself in an adulterous relationship. No woman all of a sudden begins to fill her days and consume her nights with sexually destructive behavior.

Have you ever thought about how easily you can become emotionally involved with a man who is not your husband? Whether married or single, this question is for you. Do you realize that your emotions are powerful influencers?

Your emotions and feelings can take over and dominate you, especially when it comes to sinful decisions. Just imagine how many "emotional affairs" take place at work, at the gym, and even at church. Yet in your mind, an "emotional affair" is dismissed because technically no physical activity has occurred and no harm has been done, so you think.

We must be aware of and understand that acts of sexual sin can and do occur long before the actual act of fornication or adultery. Let's examine some of those acts of sexual sin.

Act One: Entering the mind.

James says, "But each one is tempted when he is carried away and entice by his own lust" (Jas 1:14). Every sinful act is first carried out in the mind. This is the place where you could gain control, stop the foolishness before it gets out of hand, repent, and ask God for forgiveness. However, this is also the place where you might just dismiss and ignore it. You can understand why a thought entering the mind can be very dangerous depending on what you do with that thought.

Act Two: Flirting with the idea.

James says, "Then when lust has conceived …" (Jas 1:15). Visualizing and imagining different scenarios that put you and an individual together means that your emotions are involved and ignited. Your emotions automatically fuel your desire for more of that visualization and imagination. You keep thinking about you and him together—together on a car ride, together at the movies, together holding hands in the park, together at the mall, together in a restaurant and on and on.

Act Three: Embracing the idea.

James continues, "It gives birth to sin …" (Jas 1:15). Your thoughts turn to rationalizing or downplaying the sexual sin. Perhaps your marriage has grown cold and sour. Your husband does not appreciate you or rarely if ever does anything romantic. You tell yourself your marriage is over. You tell yourself you deserve better. You tell yourself that the man at work, or at the gym, or at the grocery store, always smiles and stops what he is doing to speak to you. He always shows interest in you.

Act Four: Surrendering to the idea.

James concludes, "And when sin is accomplished, it brings forth death" (Jas 1:15). The fruit of what you have been thinking and meditating on for weeks and perhaps months, becomes a reality.

Listen to the warning Jesus gives in His Sermon on the Mount:

> But I say to you that everyone who looks at a woman with lust for her has already committed adultery with her in his heart. (Matt 5:28)

Now, read it again with emphasis added:

> But I say to you that everyone [*man or woman*] who looks at a woman [*or a man*] with lust for her [*or him*] has already committed adultery with her [*or him*] in his [*or her*] heart. (Matt 5:28, emphasis added)

One thing is for certain, God views your sexual thoughts and imaginations as if you have committed the physical act. Only through guarding your heart, paying attention to sound doctrine and surrounding yourself with people who will keep you accountable can you avoid the otherwise inevitable.

Below are three resolutions, with supporting Scriptures, that every transformed woman of God should implement in her life immediately. They are Regard, Reject, and Remove.

Resolution One: REGARD the Word as precious and valuable.

> For the word of God is alive and active. Sharper than any double-edged sword, it penetrates even to dividing soul and spirit, joints and marrow; it judges the thoughts and attitudes of the heart. (Heb 4:12)

> All Scripture is God-breathed and is useful for teaching, rebuking, correcting and training in righteousness, so that the servant of God may be thoroughly equipped for every good work. (2 Tim 3:16–17)

> Therefore everyone who hears these words of mine and puts them into practice is like a wise man who built his house on the rock. (Matt 7:24)

> But prove yourselves doers of the Word, and not merely hearers who delude themselves. (Jas 1:22)

One sure way to begin to head in the direction of an unhinged woman is to stop valuing the Word of God. Stop hiding it in your heart. Stop being satisfied with it. Stop regarding it as the final authority in your life.

Resolution Two: REJECT situations that require moral compromise.

Like the young man in the father's story, King David also put himself in a compromising situation that led to adultery with Bathsheba. Notice the similarities between the choices made by the young man in Proverbs 7 and King David in 2 Samuel 11:1–17:

The Young Man **Proverbs 7:8–22**	**King David** **2 Samuel 11:1–17**
• chose to be out at a late hour (v. 9) • chose to walk near the home of an adulteress (v. 8) • chose to allow himself to be tempted sexually (v. 13) • chose to ignore the obvious signs (v. 21) • chose to believe seductive flattery (v. 21) • chose to pursue his sexual	• chose to stay in Jerusalem when the kings went out to battle (v. 1) • chose to watch a woman bathing from his rooftop (v. 2) • chose to pursue a woman who was not his wife (v. 3) • chose to have sexual relations with a woman who was not his wife (v. 4)

• impulses (v. 22) • chose to take what was not his (v. 22) • chose to end his life albeit unknowingly (v. 22)	• chose to use her husband to cover up his adultery (vv. 6–13) • chose to cause the death of her husband to solidify the coverup (vv. 14–17)

Resolution Three: REMOVE continually inward carnality.

Carnality refers to the things in your life that oppose, interfere with, and disconnect you from hearing, internalizing, and obeying the Word of God consistently. Any attitude or action that gives way to fleshly desires and interest over biblical truth is the result of carnality. Any speech or habit that reflects a way of living contrary to biblical truth is carnality.

In this regard, notice the similarities between David's prayer and Paul's admonishment:

David Said	Paul Said
"Who can discern his errors? Acquit me of hidden faults. Also keep back Your servant from presumptuous sins. Let them not rule over me. Then I shall be blameless, and I shall be acquitted of great transgression. Let the words of my mouth and the meditations of my heart be acceptable in Your sight, O Lord, my Rock and my Redeemer." (Ps 19:12–14)	"Lay aside the old self which is being corrupted in accordance with the lust of deceit, and that you be renewed in the spirit of your mind, and put on the new self which in the likeness of God has been created in righteousness and holiness of the truth." (Eph 4:23–24)

Dear Sis

Are you aware that your choice of clothes and the way you wear them automatically communicates something about you? Before you open your mouth, before you disclose anything about yourself, your attire has already spoken on your behalf. Your outward appearance and how you display it can bring to the surface and expose flaws and weaknesses in your character. It can even divulge the sensitive matters of your heart such as attention-seeking, worldliness, and the prideful desire to flaunt certain parts of your body.

Instead, your attire should communicate a gentle and quiet heart attitude that is "precious in the sight of God" (1 Pet 3:4).

As a transformed woman of God, you must always consider the reason why you wear what you wear. The fact that the heart is deceitful and desperately wicked makes answering that question all the more difficult sometimes. It requires you to think once, think twice, and then once more when purchasing clothes. What message are you sending through your attire? What message do you want your attire to send? Is your attire saying something you don't want communicated? Or worse, are your clothes and the way you choose to wear them presenting you in an overtly sexual manner?

Paul told Timothy that women should "adorn themselves with proper clothing, modestly and discreetly, not with braided hair and gold or pearls or costly garments, but rather by means of good works, as is proper for women making a claim to godliness" (1 Tim 2:9–10).

Although you may be a godly woman who is continually trying to cultivate holiness in your life, you are not immune to making sinful choices. Sometimes it takes only one poor choice to utterly devastate your life and send you down a path you never intended for yourself and, more importantly, God never intended for you.

What Are Your Thoughts?
1. What stood out to you or caused you to raise an eyebrow in this chapter?

2. What do you think Solomon meant when he said we should bind the Word on our fingers and write it on the tablet of our heart (Prov 7:3)?

3. The world says, "You should be able to wear whatever you want to wear. Body image is key and clothes should accentuate your best features, What you wear should make you feel good; If certain clothes represent your personality, go for it! No one has the right to tell you what you should and should not wear." For a transformed woman of God, what's wrong with these statements?

4. Knowing that there are women, young and older, who desire/hunt for "the precious life," how should you teach your son about the kind of woman he should desire to marry?

5. Given the fact that we live in a "freedom to express yourself" society, how will you teach your daughter or the young ladies in your life about modesty?

6. How will you caution the young and older women in your life about adopting the world's standards for how they should dress?

On a Personal Note

What are you doing to ensure that your attire reflects a woman making a claim to godliness (2 Tim 2:10)?

CHAPTER 5

Jezebel and Athaliah: A Royal Rogue Empire

(1 Kings 16:29–34; 2 Kings 8:26; 11)

> Their throat is an open grave,
> with their tongues they keep deceiving,
> the poison of asps is under their lips,
> whose mouth is full of cursing and bitterness;
> their feet are swift to shed blood,
> destruction and misery are in their paths,
> and the path of peace they have not known.
> There is no fear of God before their eyes.
>
> Romans 3:13–18

Queen Athaliah had royal blood running through her veins. She was the granddaughter of a king, the daughter of a king, the wife of a king, the mother of a king, and before her gory, tragic death, she herself became the first and only woman to reign as queen over Judah, ruling for six years.

To understand Athaliah, we must first consider her mother, Jezebel. Five characteristics immediately come to mind when I think about Jezebel that would be beneficial to examine with you:

- She had an infamous name.

- She had an infamous life.
- She had an infamous temper.
- She had an infamous death.
- She had an infamous legacy.

Jezebel had an infamous name.

The name *Jezebel* has for millennia past and will for millennia future be synonymous with pure evil. It represents wickedness of the worst kind. It is a derogatory name. It is an insulting name. It is a name that is associated with wretchedness, harm, and danger. It is a name that evokes fear and terror in one's heart.

Jezebel is the only woman's name mentioned in the Book of Revelation, and like her Old Testament counterpart, she was also engaged in evil activity:

> But I have this against you, that you tolerate the woman Jezebel, who calls herself a prophetess, and she teaches and leads My bondservants astray so that they commit acts of immorality and eat things sacrificed to idols. (Rev 2:20)

Shockingly, the name *Jezebel* means "chaste, and free from carnal connection." Chaste means moral, virtuous, pure, and restrained. Clearly, Jezebel completely contradicted and misrepresented the very meaning of her own name. She also contradicted and misrepresented womanhood in general. Far from being a "helper suitable" to her husband (Gen 2:18), she dominated, manipulated, and controlled her husband (1 Kgs 21). Far from opening "her mouth in wisdom" (Prov 31:26), she opened her mouth in lies and deception and incited her husband to do all manner of evil (1 Kgs 21:25). Far from being a fruitful vine within her house (Ps 128:3), her feet ran to evil and were swift to shed innocent blood (Isa 59:7).

Jezebel had an infamous life.

Jezebel has been likened to a female version of Judas ... but on steroids. You cannot get anymore unhinged than Jezebel. She was the quintessential unhinged woman in the Bible, the worst of the worst.

Jezebel was a devout worshiper of Baal, which is not surprising given the fact that her father was King Ethbaal whose name meant "a man of Baal." She grew up in Baal worship. After she became the wife of King Ahab, the seventh king of Israel, the Bible says Ahab:

- went to serve Baal and worship him (1 Kgs 16:31)
- built an altar for Baal in the house of Baal in Samaria (1 Kgs 16:32)
- made the Asherah, which were idols carved to stimulate worship of Baal's female counterpart (1 Kgs 16:32–33)
- did more to provoke the Lord God of Israel than all the kings of Israel who were before him (1 Kgs 16:33)
- sold himself to do evil in the sight of the Lord, because Jezebel his wife incited him (1 Kgs 21:25)
- acted very abominably in following idols (1 Kgs 21:26)

It was not enough for Jezebel to influence her weak husband to worship Baal; she wanted to force all of Israel to recognize Baal as god and worship him. To clear a path towards nationwide Baal worship, she had thousands of the prophets of the Lord put to death. The Bible says Obadiah, one of Ahab's officials, "took a hundred prophets and hid them by fifties in a cave and provided them with bread" (1 Kgs 18:4). They remained hidden in the cave for the duration of the killing spree.

Jezebel met and conquered many unwanted situations with deadly force, literally! She had no problem discarding anyone who got in her way or posed a threat to the royal agenda. Naboth was one such tragedy.

Jezebel had an infamous temper.

Naboth owned a vineyard in Samaria near Ahab's palace. Ahab set his heart on purchasing the vineyard, but Naboth refused to sell the land (Num 36:7–8; Lev 25:23–28). So, Ahab returned to his house and laid on his bed "sullen and vexed … turned away his face and ate no food" because Naboth would not sell him his land (1 Kgs 21:4). Being an Israelite, Ahab most likely knew that what Naboth told him was part of the Mosaic Law. Therefore, nothing could ever be said or done to reverse Naboth's refusal to sell him the land. Enter Jezebel, who told Ahab, "Are you king or what? Get up! Eat, drink and be merry! You will have the land, I'll see to it!" (1 Kgs 21:7, emphasis added).

Forging letters with the king's signature, Jezebel wrote, "To the elders and to the nobles," ordering a call to fast. False charges of blaspheme were brought up against Naboth, according to 1 Kings 21:13. Then, after word was sent to Jezebel that Naboth had been stoned to death, she informed Ahab and told him, "Arise, take possession of the vineyard of Naboth … for he was not alive but dead" (1 Kgs 21:15). And if it wasn't enough to take the life of innocent Naboth, his two sons were also murdered so that an heir could not lay claim to his vineyard.

Thanks to Jezebel, a mere desire of King Ahab resulted in the slaughter of three innocent men (2 Kgs 9:26). Jezebel promised. Jezebel delivered!

Elijah was a prophet of the Lord God and therefore a great enemy of Ahab and Jezebel. He prophesied and warned Ahab that there would be no rain for a period of time. At the end of a three-year drought, Elijah decided to challenge the prophets of Baal to demonstrate that the God of Israel was the only true and living God. Two altars were prepared, each with an animal to be sacrificed. The prophets of Baal were given the first opportunity to call on their god to produce fire for the altar. After crying out to their god, severely cutting themselves as was their custom, and some taunting from Elijah, the better part of the day had gone by without response.

Elijah then called on the Lord God: "Answer me, O Lord, answer me that this people may know that You O Lord are God and that You have turned their heart back again" (1 Kgs 18:37). Immediately, the fire of the Lord "fell and consumed the burnt offering and the wood and the stones and the dust, and licked up the water that was in the trench" (1 Kgs 18:38).

When the people saw what had happened, they fell on their faces and confessed that the Lord was God. Elijah then had the prophets of Baal brought "to the brook Kishon" (1 Kgs 18:39), where he killed them.

Ahab returned home and told Jezebel all that had happened to the prophets of Baal (1 Kgs 19:1). Needless to say, this news did not sit well with her. It's not hard to imagine the sharp animosity she harbored against Elijah. Her response was what you would come to expect from a woman who seemed to have murder in her DNA.

In her rage, Jezebel swore that she would kill Elijah by the exact same time on the very next day. She had a vicious temper. Her heart was dominated by darkness. She knew nothing about being civil. Anything that angered her was dealt with in the most extreme and cruel manner. Certain that she would carry out her threat, Elijah "ran for his life" (1 Kgs 19:3).

Jezebel had an infamous death.

Although Elijah ran quite a distance from Jezebel, the Lord not only protected him but used him to confront Ahab. God's prophet pronounced judgment on Ahab and Jezebel for their egregious sins, beginning with a rhetorical question, "Have you murdered and also taken possession?" He followed that with the details of the severe judgment to be leveled against them:

- Ahab was going to die (1 Kgs 21:19).
- Ahab's blood would be licked up by dogs (1 Kgs 21:19).
- Evil would be brought upon Ahab (1 Kgs 21:21).

- Every male would be cut off from Ahab, both bond or free, and eaten by dogs or birds. It would bear a resemblance to what took place in the house of Jeroboam and Baasha (1 Kgs 14:11; 16:4; 21:21–22).
- Jezebel would be eaten by dogs in Jezreel (1 Kgs 21:23).

The judgment announced by Elijah was actually carried out by King Jehu, who was originally one of Ahab's officials. After being anointed king of Israel and told by God that he was to "strike the house of Ahab" his master as judgment for the deaths of the servants of the Lord, Jehu set out on his new mission (2 Kgs 9:7) and faithfully carried out God's command to annihilate the house of Ahab.

Jezebel, being one of the last vestiges of the horrible house of Ahab, somehow received word that Jehu was coming for her. She must have known her death was near. She prepared herself to look as physically attractive and queenly as she could. No doubt expecting to have a proper burial fit for a queen, she proceeded to paint her eyes and adorn her head (2 Kgs 9:30). Yet, no amount of attire or makeup could have covered up her ugly, murderous heart.

So steeped in evil, Jezebel did not once consider the life she had lived. She felt no sorrow, no remorse, and no grief because of her evil ways. She did not even consider the people she had murdered, the lives she had ruined, the schemes she had devised, the lies she had told, or the monster she was. Even in her last moments of life, she thought about what she had always thought about: herself. She was a queen, and she wanted to go out looking like a queen.

When God speaks, it is as good as done. God had already said that Jezebel would be eaten by dogs. Apparently, King Ahab did not inform his wife of her horrific judgment as told by Elijah. Ahab told her everything else but was too much of a coward to tell her how she was going to die.

All dressed up in her queenly regalia, Jezebel looked out the window as Jehu entered the gate and insultingly spoke what would be her last words: "Is it well, Zimri, your master's murderer?" (2 Kgs 9:31) By calling Jehu "Zimri," she was implying that he was not a legitimate king but nothing more than a conspirator and that his reign would be cut short just as Zimri's was cut short forty-five years earlier (1 Kgs 16:9–15).

Jezebel was immediately thrown from a window by her own officials. Her blood spattered the walls and horses when she hit the ground. Her body was trampled underfoot by the horses and then, just as Elijah prophesied, Jezebel was devoured by a pack of dogs. These dogs are better understood to be scavengers, which was why only the skull, feet and palms of her hands were found later when the officials tried to retrieve her body for burial (2 Kgs 9:33–35).

Jezebel suffered a violent death. She lived a cursed life, and she died cursed by God for her wickedness. Isn't it ironic that the one to whom she devoted her life could not save her in her most dire time of need? Isn't it ironic that the thing she called god could not provide her a proper burial or prevent her death altogether? How utterly sobering these words about her are:

> Therefore, they returned and told him. And he said, "This is the word of the Lord, which He spoke by His servant Elijah the Tishbite, saying, 'In the property of Jezreel the dogs shall eat the flesh of Jezebel; and the corpse of Jezebel shall be as dung on the face of the field in the property of Jezreel, so they cannot say, "This is Jezebel."'" (2 Kgs 9:36–37)

If only Jezebel had humbled herself and repented of her sinful life, perhaps she would have come to know that:

> The idols of the nations are but silver and gold, the work of man's hands. They have mouths, but they do not see; they have ears, but they do not hear; nor is there any breath at all in their mouths. Those who make them will be like them, yes, everyone who trusts in them. (Ps 135:15–18)

Jezebel had an infamous legacy.

When you hear the word "legacy," you may think of an outstanding mark or influence a person has left after they die. You may think of the result or impact the deceased had on the people closest to them and even on the world at large. Legacy is sometimes defined as what people remember most about you or what people valued the most about your life. It has the connotation of something good and positive, worthwhile and noteworthy. A legacy is what people strive to carry on into the next generation.

It is extremely difficult to use "legacy" in the same sentence when speaking of Jezebel, knowing the kind of person she was. Sadly, even vile, evil people leave a legacy. Hers was a legacy of idol worship, violence, murder, and I could go on and on, but you get the idea.

Unfortunately, Jezebel's legacy began long before she died. The Bible says that her husband and two sons did evil in the sight of the Lord. They also served Baal and provoked God to anger (1 Kgs 16:30; 22:52–53; 2 Kgs 3:2–3). These verses say it all. They provide undeniable evidence of Jezebel's handiwork. Her evil ways influenced her husband and were ingrained in the lives of her two sons. Coming from a pedigree like that, is it any wonder that Jezebel's only daughter Athaliah not only repeated her mother's evil ways but took them a step further?

Is it possible that someone could be more evil than Jezebel? Yes, her daughter! Even the Bible directly calls her "the wicked Athaliah" (2 Chron 24:7). No such statement is made of Jezebel, although she was very wicked.

However, Athaliah's most vicious and brutal act was done when she was a grandmother.

I feel so blessed to be called grandmother. One of the greatest high points of 2020 was when my youngest daughter gave birth to a baby boy (Wyatt Ebenezer) and made me one. As you can imagine, I have held my grandson countless times. I have coddled him, kissed him, fed him, rocked him to sleep, sung to him, prayed over him, read to him, pronounced "grandmother" to him, and laughed with him (I love to hear him laugh) countless times. The sheer joy he brings to me is immeasurable. The love I have for him is immeasurable. The very, very rare times I have not been able to babysit him, due to dealing with my own journey to better health, were heartbreaking times. At the writing of this book, he turned one year old. I look forward to watching him grow up and to grow in the grace and knowledge of the Lord Jesus Christ!

That's why a grandmother who had her own grandsons murdered is a level of wickedness I cannot even comprehend. How could a woman be so vicious as to kill her own grandchildren?

Coming from a long line of evil doers, Athaliah, like her mother, was also steeped in evil. She was the wife of Jehoram, King of Judah, who the Bible says, "did evil in the sight of the Lord" (2 Kgs 8:18). She counseled her son "to do wickedly" (2 Chron 22:3). And yet, what she did to gain control of the throne and become the reigning queen in Judah places her in a category of infamy above that of her mother. For no other woman mentioned in the Bible, including Jezebel, had her own grandchildren slaughtered.

After her son, King Ahaziah, was killed in battle, Athaliah apparently had her sights already set on the throne to become queen. She had ruled her husband and then her son from behind the scenes, and now that both were dead, she saw an opportunity to rule openly as queen of Judah. The only problem was that she would have to get rid of all of the rightful heirs to the throne — that is, her very own progeny, her grandsons:

> When Athaliah the mother of Ahaziah saw that her son was dead, she rose and destroyed all the royal offspring. But Jehosheba, the daughter of King Joram, sister of Ahaziah, took Joash the son of Ahaziah and stole him from among the king's sons who were being put to death, and placed him and his nurse in the bedroom. So they hid him from Athaliah, and he was not put to death. (2 Kgs 11:1–2)

Praise be to God, He always has a remnant. As verse 3 then reassures us, thanks to his aunt, Athaliah's grandson Joash "was hidden with her in the house of the Lord six years, while Athaliah was reigning over the land" (2 Kgs 11:3).

By the time Athaliah found out about her one remaining grandson nearly seven years later, he was being crowned King of Judah. He had an army of protection to make sure nothing happened to him while being crowned (2 Kgs 11:5–11). Jehoiada, the high priest, ordered to have anyone put to death who entered the house during the coronation (2 Kgs 11:8; 2 Chron 23:7).

Athaliah "came to the people in the house of the Lord." She saw the crowd gathered and heard the musicians playing and people singing and shouting, "Long live the king!" In an angry act of protest, she tore her clothes and screamed, "Treason! Treason!" (2 Kgs 11:14). Because she had entered the house of the Lord, she was immediately seized, and "when she arrived at the horses entrance, she was put to death there" (2 Kgs 11:16).

Like Mother, Like Daughter

Right down to her gruesome death, Athaliah was like her mother, for she too was no doubt trampled by horses. So ended the wicked life of Athaliah. Interestingly, as 2 Kings 11:20 records, "So all the people of the land rejoiced, and the city was quiet. For they had put Athaliah to death with the sword at the king's house." We do not read of anyone rejoicing when Jezebel died. Athaliah is the only woman and the only royal whose death triggered rejoicing and celebration! Clearly, Athaliah was even more wicked than her treacherous mother.

Lois And Eunice

Almost a millennia later, another mother and daughter duo is mentioned in the text of Scripture. They were two of the most godly women in the Bible. Their names were Lois and Eunice. Eunice had a son whose name was Timothy.

Not a lot is said in Scripture about Lois and Eunice, but what is said speaks volumes. We first learn about the two godly women and their direct influence on Timothy from the apostle Paul. He mentions them by name and identifies Lois as Timothy's grandmother. As he writes in his second pastoral letter to Timothy, "I am reminded of your sincere faith, which first lived in your grandmother Lois and in your mother Eunice and, I am persuaded, now lives in you also" (2 Tim 1:5).

This reference to Lois is the only place the term "grandmother" is used in Scripture. God wanted us to know that Lois was a grandmother. God wanted us to know that the sincere faith found in Timothy began in her, his grandmother.

So many times, I have heard testimonies from people that their grandmother was the one who taught them the Word of God. It was their grandmother who took them to church. It was their grandmother who constantly prayed for them. I can imagine how many times Timothy, one of the greatest young men in Scripture, must have spoken of his grandmother and her involvement in his spiritual life.

Lois took the Scriptures seriously, and her love for the Lord and faith in Jesus Christ compelled her to teach them to her grandson. She did not leave teaching of Scripture to him solely to his mother.

Eunice was a Jewish believer and, according to Luke, had married a Greek (Acts 16:1–3). The fact that there is no further mention of Timothy's father could mean that he had not been converted to Christianity and had no part in Timothy's spiritual growth.

With no male influence or spiritual leadership in the family, what Lois and Eunice accomplished was all the more remarkable. Perhaps both women got saved on Paul's first missionary journey. Whatever the case, before they became Christians, they were faithful Jewish women teaching Timothy the Old Testament Scriptures. Both continued studying and learning the Scriptures, and both passed on that knowledge to Timothy.

When God moved in Timothy's heart, what helped him have a desire to know Christ and a desire to build godly character? It was the teachings of his grandmother and his mother! Together, these two God-fearing women established in Timothy a solid foundation of faith. Faith that was carried along and built upon so much so that Paul took notice of Timothy and wanted Timothy to accompany him on his journeys in spreading the gospel (Acts 16:2–3).

In a time when numerous women are rushing to scale the steps leading to a pulpit, to stand behind a podium and "preach," it is refreshing and such a blessing to be encouraged by a mother and grandmother who faithfully taught the Word of God to their young son. From their home, they lived out the Word of God and used their powerful influence on him to train him in the Word. They used their gift of teaching, not in contradiction, but in obedience to the Scriptures. Because of Lois and Eunice's faithfulness, Timothy:

- was well spoken of by the elders in Lystra and Iconium (Acts 16:2)
- was an evangelist and accompanied Paul serving as a missionary
- was referred to by Paul as a "son" in the faith (2 Tim 1:2; 2:1)
- became the pastor of Ephesus (1 Tim 1:1–3)
- was with Paul when he wrote numerous New Testament letters (2 Corinthians, Philippians, Colossians, 1 & 2 Thessalonians, and Philemon)

This faithfulness on Lois's and Eunice's part on behalf of Timothy reminds me of the psalmist who said:

> But the lovingkindness of the Lord is from everlasting to everlasting on those who fear Him, and His righteousness to children's children, to those who keep His covenant and remember His precepts to do them. (Ps 103:17)

What a stark difference between the lives of Lois and Eunice and those of Jezebel and Athaliah:

Lois and Eunice	**Jezebel and Athaliah**
Godly	Wicked
True worshipers	Idolatrous
Built godly heritage	Built destructive heritage
Sincere in faith	Deceptive
Spiritually influential	Threatening
Obedient	Proud
Lived righteously	Lived savagely
Servants of God	Enemies of God
Loved the Lord	Rejected the Lord
Rightly handled the Word of God	Mocked the Word of God
Courageous	Overbearing
Selfless	Heartless
Loved God's people	Murdered God's people
Used by God	Cursed by God

Lois and Eunice, two of the most godly women in Scripture, had no way of knowing how far reaching their legacy of faith would extend nor the profound impact Timothy's life would have on the church for generations and generations to come.

Dear Sis

You may be wondering, can any lessons be learned from such heartless and cruel women as Jezebel and Athaliah?

One obvious lesson is that wickedness will always be met with divine retribution! Jezebel's demise was foretold, Athaliah's was not. Yet, both received severe judgment from the hand of God for the evil that dwelled in their hearts and characterized their lives.

> For the ways of a man are before the eyes of the Lord, and He watches all his paths. His own iniquities will capture the wicked and he will be held with the cords of his sin. (Prov 5:21–22)

Another and more important lesson to be learned is that there is only one way to live life and that is in the fear of the Lord God.

What Are Your Thoughts?

1. What stood out to you or caused you to raise an eyebrow in this chapter?

2. What do we learn about a woman's capacity to influence from Jezebel and Athaliah and from Lois and Eunice?

3. Both Jezebel and Athaliah would have been praised by the feminist movement in our culture today. They would be viewed as powerful role models, glass ceiling breakers, not held back by men. How can mothers of daughters train them to be successful and excellent in their work while still maintaining respect for men and the role God has given to men?

4. How can a Christian woman use her position of influence, power, and strength while also maintaining a meek and quiet spirit and

following the mandates of Scripture found in 1 Timothy 3:11; Proverbs 11:16; 14:1; 31:30; and Colossians 3:18?

On a Personal Note

Have you acted like Jezebel in your marriage, trying to control your husband and lead the relationship? What steps should you take to reverse that behavior?

PART TWO

TRANSFORMED WOMEN

CHAPTER 6

The Samaritan Woman: A Divine Work

(John 4:1–42)

> You did not choose Me but I chose you,
> and appointed you that you would go
> and bear fruit …
>
> John 15:16

Even if you did not grow up in the church like I did, you've probably heard the story of the Samaritan woman. It is a well-known story, filled with unique and even surprising events. For example, it represents one of the rare occasions when Jesus was alone during His three-year ministry. Usually, He was surrounded by multitudes of people who observed Him teaching His disciples, healing the sick and responding to the Pharisees' nefarious questions. Yet, the Samaritan woman had an encounter with Jesus when not even His disciples were around (John 4:8).

Another shocking fact about this story is that Jesus not only chose to have a conversation with a Samaritan but a Samaritan *woman*. It was uncommon for respectable Jewish men to speak to women in public in that culture; it was considered a breach of religious etiquette. Rabbis certainly did not speak to women openly and, in fact, Jewish men did not talk to the women of their own family in public.

Yet, Scripture is clear that Jesus purposely went to where the Samaritan woman would be and initiated a conversation with her:

> He left Judea and went away again into Galilee. And He had to pass through Samaria. So He came to a city of Samaria called Sychar, near the parcel of ground that Jacob gave to his son Joseph; and Jacob's well was there. So Jesus, being wearied from His journey, was sitting thus by the well. It was about the sixth hour. (John 4:4–6)

This encounter took place during Jesus' journey from Judea to Galilee. Samaria was a region located between the two regions and was the shorter route. Nevertheless, most Jews took a longer route through the city of Perea, east of the Jordan River, to avoid entering Samaria and having any contact with Samaritans. If you know anything about the relationship between Jews and Samaritans, you know they had a sharp hatred for one another. Jews despised Samaritans.

What caused this hatred between the two groups? As Bruce Barton explains in his *Life Application New Testament Commentary*,

> In the Old Testament days, when the northern kingdom of Israel, with its capital at Samaria, fell to the Assyrians, many Jews were deported to Assyria. King Sargon of Assyria repopulated the northern kingdom with captives from other lands to settle the territory and keep the peace (2 Kgs 17:24). These captives eventually intermarried with the few Jews who remained in the land to form a mixed race of people who became known as Samaritans. The Jews who lived in the southern kingdom felt betrayed by the Jews in the northern kingdom due to their intermarriage with

foreigners. They hated the Samaritans because they were not pure Jews.[1]

Intermarrying with pagan, idolatrous, half-Gentile people was an ongoing point of contention and fueled the Jews' animosity towards the Samaritans. Moreover, the Samaritans established worship at Mt. Gerizim, while the Jews worshiped in Jerusalem. Adding to the hostility was the fact that the Samaritans only regarded the first five books of the Old Testament (The Pentateuch) as Scripture and disregarded the rest.

Despite the severe tension between the two groups, Jesus traveled directly through Samaria on His way to Galilee. He crossed racial and cultural lines, demonstrating that He did not allow the social norms of the day to shape His attitude and dictate His actions. After reaching the city of Sychar, His disciples traveled a little further into town to purchase food (John 4:5). Perhaps following Jesus's example, they also did not allow the social norms of the day to shape their attitudes, which would have prevented their interaction with the Samaritan people.

One of the most stunning aspects of the story is the woman Jesus intentionally pursued. It wasn't just that she was a Samaritan. Other factors were in play:

- She was immoral.
- She was despised.
- She was confused yet willing to engage.

The Samaritan woman was immoral.

Think about it, the Samaritan woman had been married five times, and all five marriages had ended in divorce. There is no question she was an

---

[1] Dr. Bruce Barton, *Life Application New Testament Commentary* (Carol Stream, IL: Tyndale House Publishers, Inc., 2001), 388.

immoral woman. She was unapologetically immoral. She lived up to no one's expectations. She lived life the way she wanted.

You have to wonder why she was married and divorced so many times. Could any of those divorces been due to unfaithfulness? The Samaritans acknowledged the first five books of the Bible, which means they would have been aware of the Mosaic Law that allowed for divorce only in the case of infidelity. The one reasonable and most likely answer for the multiple severed marriages was that the Samaritan woman was an adulterous woman. She may have even been a prostitute.

She knew the Mosaic Law and the consequences of breaking that law. Yet, neither kept her from being the kind of woman she was. Sadly, the marriage covenant itself did nothing to curtail her immoral lifestyle.

At the time when Jesus met her, she was not married but living in an adulterous relationship (John 4:18), possibly heading toward marriage number six. If she were a celebrity in modern America, she would rank right alongside media personality and socialite Kim Kardashian who has been married three times, and Jennifer Lopez and supermodel Christie Brinkley who have both been married four times. Shockingly, Elizabeth Taylor was married eight times; however, Zsa Zsa Gabor beats all of them having been married a whopping nine times. But in New Testament times, needless to say, Jesus' seeking out a conversation with a woman whose reputation was marred by immorality was no doubt viewed as scandalous.

Furthermore, if Jesus had not met her that day, there was no indication that she would have changed her way of life. As we will soon find out, only faith in the Lord Jesus Christ changes (transforms) a person.

Jesus is not only attracted to faith, He is the giver of faith. Oftentimes, during His earthly ministry, He drew attention to the faith of each individual He encountered (Mark 2:1–5; 5:24–34). One such occasion was when He encountered a woman at a dinner party. Just like the Samaritan woman, she had lived an immoral life and was known as a woman "of the city" (Luke 7:36–50).

THE SAMARITAN WOMAN: A DIVINE WORK

The dinner, hosted by Simon the Pharisee, was underway when a particular sort of woman showed up and crashed the party. She invited herself when she found out that Jesus was there. Unlike any of the other guests, this woman brought something to give to Jesus. Her gift and the manner in which it was presented became the focus of the evening. By the end of the story, Simon received a stern warning, the woman received forgiveness, and the guests were stunned by what they had witnessed.

When the woman approached Jesus, she immediately began weeping. Unable to compose herself, her tears began saturating His feet. Remember, in that culture, people did not sit in chairs around a dining table as we do in America. People reclined on the floor around a long table about the height of what we call a coffee table. In a reclining position, their legs and feet would be exposed. This is how the woman was able to stand behind Jesus "at His feet, weeping" (Luke 7:38). When she attempted to dry His feet with her hair, she began kissing them. Her tears and love for Him evidenced a deep sorrow over her sin.

Grateful to be near Jesus, she felt compelled to anoint His feet. According to Bruce Barton, "Many Jewish women wore a small perfume flask on a cord around their neck. This jar of perfume would have been highly valued by this woman."[2] Yet nothing was too costly to show honor, appreciation and thanksgiving to Jesus. As she poured the beautiful perfume on His feet, her eyes continued to fill up with tears.

Repeatedly kissing, weeping, and anointing the feet of Jesus brought out the vitriol in Simon. In his heart, he criticized and denounced Jesus as a fraud and the woman as despicable. What Simon did not realize was that Jesus heard every word he "said to himself" (Luke 7:39).

Speaking to Simon, Jesus told a parable about a moneylender and two debtors. One debtor owed considerably more than the other. Surprisingly, the moneylender expunged both debts. Jesus asked Simon which debtor

---

[2] Ibid., 280.

would love the moneylender more? Simon answered, "The one who had been forgiven more" (Luke 7:43).

Jesus used the parable to contrast Simon's self-righteous attitude and failure to perform basic acts of hospitality with the woman's overwhelming acts of love and gratitude. Simon received a warning while the woman received a commendation and blessing. She was completely exonerated of her sins, which were many. She had placed her faith in Jesus and was no longer "a woman of the city," as Simon knew her to be. Jesus transformed her life!

Speaking directly to the woman, Jesus made two declarations: "Your sins have been forgiven" (Luke 7:48) and "Your faith has saved you, go in peace" (Luke 7:50). Those must have been some of the sweetest words she had ever heard!

Faith is also what the Samaritan woman at the well so desperately needed. She came to get water (John 4:7a), but she really needed what only Jesus could give her: faith in Him!

The Samaritan woman was despised.

This was not a woman who attracted girlfriends. She was no doubt viewed as repulsive and offensive. Her body language and flagrant flirting set the women in the village on edge. It did not matter if the man was married or single, she was always doing her thing. Living with a man who was not her husband put the Samaritan woman squarely in the immoral category. She had also gone through not one or two but five husbands. She was a serial adulterer, a perpetual ex-wife, an outcast!

Just imagine if you were the sister or mother of one of those men she had cheated on. Just imagine the hurt you would feel for your son or brother who has been messed over by this kind of woman. It's not too difficult to understand why she was despised and ostracized. Her horrible reputation preceded her, as it was widespread knowledge the kind of woman she was and her dealings with men. Although she was able to catch the eye of a man, deep down inside, she was probably a lonely woman.

Drawing water was a common, daily task that women did together. Women did not travel alone but in groups for safety reasons. Meeting at the well provided an opportunity to catch up with friends and family. It was a social outlet that women looked forward to and expected.

The Samaritan woman traveled alone. She chose to go to a well in Sychar. Scholars have identified wells that were much closer that she could have gone to. Why travel further than was necessary? Why did she schedule her time to arrive "about the sixth hour" (John 4:6)? The sixth hour was in the middle of the day. Women did not travel in the heat of the day but rather in the early morning or early evening hours when the temperatures would be cooler. Most likely, she chose that time because she knew the women of the town would not be around (Gen 24:11).

I can imagine the sun and heat did not matter to her as long as she could be alone. Most likely, she was aware of how others felt about her. Most likely, women were uncomfortable around her and kept their distance.

It is likely that the Samaritan woman wanted to avoid all of it: the side-eyed looks, the whispering, the gossip, the innuendos, the scorn, the disparaging remarks, and the feelings of guilt and shame. Perhaps she went at the sixth hour expecting to draw the water she needed without distractions or confrontations.

Perhaps the whole scene felt strange to her, as she approached the well. The first thing she would have noticed was a Jewish man sitting at the well. As was mentioned earlier, Jews detested Samaritans and the feeling was mutual. Jews would avoid traveling in the Samaritan region at all costs. That a Jewish man was in Samaria, resting at a place where women gather to draw water, would have been cause for alarm. I doubt if she had ever seen such a sight. Men were not the ones who drew water from wells, that was considered women's work (Gen 24:11).

Furthermore, because He was "wearied from His journey" (John 4:6), Jesus may have been sitting in a slumped position, visibly fatigued, exhausted, and perhaps even sweaty. Remember, He was fully man and subjected Himself to some of the same things to which any other man was subjected. Samaria was hot. Traveling from Judea to Galilee was not a casual stroll but a hard, strenuous journey. Jesus was tired and thirsty, and He probably looked like it.

Lastly, the Samaritan woman's expectation was to be alone while drawing water. At the sight of a Jewish man sitting on the well, she may have considered turning around and heading in the opposite direction. Perhaps a number of questions flooded her mind. What was he doing there? Was he injured or sick? Was he deranged?

> Jesus said to her, "Give Me a drink." For His disciples had gone away into the city to buy food. (John 4:7b–8)

The Samaritan woman was confused yet willing to engage.

It is also interesting to note that the Samaritan woman did not seem to be a bitter woman. Sinful choices and the ensuing consequences sometimes result in a bitter heart attitude. That root of bitterness continues to grow and is fueled by one negative experience after another. Moreover, a bitter heart attitude causes a person to view all of life through the lens of their unpleasant circumstances. Bitterness cannot be defeated until one is willing to confess it and turn to Christ. Only through Christ can bitterness be overcome.

I can imagine the Samaritan woman had plenty of negative experiences in her life; however she did not seem to be bitter about her circumstances. She did not seem to be bitter about her immoral life. She did not seem to be bitter about the way others treated her. Why do I believe this to be the case? Because she demonstrated no hostility or frustration toward Jesus when He asked her for a drink. She was confused yet willing to engage. She responded to Him when she could have ignored him.

Because she responded, she had a one-on-one encounter with the Savior of the world. She did not know it yet, but the King of kings and Lord of lords was sitting in her presence, inviting her into conversation, and she entered in:

> Therefore the Samaritan woman said to Him, "How is it that You, being a Jew, ask me for a drink since I am a Samaritan woman? For Jews have no dealings with Samaritans." Jesus answered and said to her, "If you knew the gift of God, and who it is who says to you, 'Give Me a drink,' you would have asked Him, and He would have given you living water." (John 4:9–10)

The "gift of God" Jesus was referring to is the Holy Spirit (John 7:37–39). The Holy Spirit indwells a person once they repent and believe in Jesus, and His presence in their heart is evidence that genuine, transforming faith has occurred. The Holy Spirit enlightens us to the truth (John 16:13–16), convicts us of sin (John 16:8), teaches us how to walk in obedience (Gal 5; Eph 5), empowers us to be an effective witness (Acts 1:8), causes us to maintain unity in the body of Christ (Phil 1:1–2), and comforts us in sorrow (John 14)—just to name a few of His beneficial attributes. However, Jesus Himself is also a gift of God and the only way to know God.

Jesus is the gift of God to a sinful world. Do you know it? Do you believe it? Do you talk about it? Jesus cannot be overlooked or dismissed. John said, "For God so loved the world that He gave His only begotten Son, that whosoever believes in Him will not perish but have everlasting life" (John 3:16). Peter said, "And there is salvation in no other name under heaven that has been given among men by which we must be saved" (Acts 4:12). Jesus Himself said, "I am the way, the truth, and the life; no one comes to the Father but through Me" (John 14:6).

Have you noticed that we are living in a time when most people are comfortable talking about God and about their "faith?" From celebrities to the neighbors next door, people speak of God openly and freely. I have heard people who hold some of the highest positions in the country talk about God and faith. I have even heard rappers who defame, demean, and defile women with their vulgar lyrics credit God for their success in the music industry. Initiating a conversation about God is not too difficult especially in the south, the so-called Bible Belt. People will talk about God.

What you won't hear are people talking about Jesus. People will talk about faith and make no mention of repentance and forgiveness granted through Christ. When Jesus is introduced into the conversation, people become uncomfortable, weird and sometimes utterly offended.

The Samaritan woman needed to recognize that the only way to have access to the gift of God, or the "living water," was through Jesus. Moreover, she must ask for it.

The very mention of living water sparked her attention all the more. Yet, she could not get past the practical matters: Jesus had no bucket to draw water, and the well was deep. Where could this living water be found, and what about the greatness of Jacob (John 4:11–12)? Jesus continued engaging her in conversation, keeping her attention on the living water by explaining that "whoever drinks of the water that I will give him shall never thirst; but the water that I will give him will become in him a well of water springing up to eternal life" (John 4:14).

Did she realize what He was telling her? Did she understand that living water was not a thing or place but a Person? Did she understand that living water is eternal life? Her response indicates she didn't: "Sir, give me this water, so I will not be thirsty nor come all the way here to draw." Once again, the Samaritan woman was distracted by practical matters: physical thirst and one less chore to deal with in her daily tasks (John 4:15).

The conversation thus far was about water. It began with Jesus asking for a drink rather than addressing her sinful lifestyle. Only after her attention was on Him, who He was and what He could give her, did Jesus deal with the proverbial "elephant in the room," namely, her sin.

Apart from a relationship with Jesus, sin is what separates us from God. Furthermore, sin gets us to believe we can't help ourselves and the way we live. Sin gets us to believe we were dealt a bad hand in life, and we are doing the best we can! Sin gets us to believe that if we feel good about something, it must be good for us. Sin gets us to believe we can do what we want to do because we control our own destiny.

Not having to deal with sin is one of the reasons "religious" people feel comfortable with their version of knowing God. They believe God understands their sinful ways. Their kind of "faith" allows them to remain who they are. Their kind of faith does not get in the way of how they view life or how they want to live life. As such, they think God is on their side, that He operates on their terms.

However, Jesus never overlooks sin. He never sweeps it under the carpet or excuses it because we are "only human." Rather, He says, "If anyone wishes to come after Me, he must deny himself and take up his cross and follow Me" (Matt 16:24). Jesus deals with sin head on. Until we can see ourselves in the light of who Christ is, until we can see our filth, wretchedness, and ruin in the light of Christ's righteousness and holiness, we cannot and will not come to Him for salvation.

With that in mind, now notice the very next thing Jesus says to the Samaritan woman: "Go, call your husband and come here" (John 4:16). With that simple command, thus Jesus began exposing her broken life. He put His finger directly on her real problem. It wasn't about a well, a bucket, drawing water, or Jacob's greatness. The woman had a sin problem, as we all do. Jesus could no longer speak about living water and how to get it until her sin was addressed.

What does this teach us about living water?

- We cannot drink from the well of living water and continue to be slaves to sin. When the Samaritan woman asked for the living water (v. 15), Jesus addressed her sin first.

- Living water conquers sin. Living water cleanses from sin. Sin must no longer hold the same power as it once did. There must be a clear demarcation between who we were before Christ and who we are after submitting to Christ. Living water establishes that demarcation.
- Living water is given by grace and through faith to all who ask for it. That Jesus "had to pass through Samaria" (v. 4) was a profound act of grace for the sole purpose of saving a woman and consequently an entire village of people (vv. 39–42).
- Living water works the same regardless of the sins we commit. Whether you have lived a life of immorality, degradation, and denouncing the existence of God, or a "good life," living water saves, restores and sets us free from the bondage of sin.

It is interesting that the Apostle John wrote about Nicodemus and the Samaritan woman back-to-back. It seems to be clear that John wants his audience and readers to grasp a powerful truth. That powerful truth is that, regardless of who we are, regardless of our status in life, regardless of how others may perceive us, we need Jesus! We need the saving grace of Jesus. Nicodemus, a respected and educated ruler, needed salvation just as much as the despised, uneducated woman of Samaria. No one needs or gets more of Jesus than anyone else. We need Him equally the same.

Stunned by Jesus's reference to her husband, the Samaritan woman simply responded, "I have no husband" (John 4:17). She said nothing further.

It's not too hard to understand why she did not want to rehash all of the sordid details of years of immoral living. It's not hard to understand why she chose not to mention five failed marriages. Nor is it hard to understand why she did not disclose the fact that she was currently living with a man. Perhaps she gave enough information hoping Jesus would move on to another subject.

He did not! Instead, He acknowledged her truthfulness and finished the rest of her sad story for her (John 4:17–18). Isn't it just like Jesus to not force her to articulate every aspect of her sinful life? He treated the woman caught in adultery in the same way (John 8:1–11). Jesus does not use sin to embarrass the sinner or weakness to embarrass the weak.

He is the same with you and me. We don't have to sort through and identify every single sin and godless act we have ever committed. In fact, if our life depended on it, we would fail. We don't even know all of the sins we have committed against God. He knows! Yet, He forgives us, in spite of us. He loves us, in spite of us. He offers Himself, in spite of us.

How Jesus treated the Samaritan woman reminded me of what happened in the story of the prodigal son. When the son finally came to his senses, after leaving home, squandering his inheritance and finding himself desiring "the pods that the swine were eating" (Luke 15:16), he was deeply repentant. He then prepared himself mentally for what he would say to his father when he returned home. I can imagine the son rehearsed it over and over. What he did not know was that his father had been watching and waiting for him to return since the day he left. As Luke 15:20 describes, "So he got up and came to his father. But while he was still a long way off, his father saw him and felt compassion for him and ran and embraced him and kissed him." Before he could complete all he had planned to say, the father ordered his servants to bring a robe, a ring, and sandals for him. He also ordered them to prepare a feast. The father wanted nothing less than a celebration for his son who was dead and had come to life, was lost and had been found (Luke 15:24)!

This story of the prodigal son represents what genuine transformation looks like. Acknowledging your sinfulness and acknowledging that you are unable to do anything about it is the beginning of the process. The prodigal son could not stay where he was and experience help from his father. He had to leave one place and go to another.

Turning from a life of sin, coming to the Father, confessing your sin, and receiving what Christ offers is true conversion and real transformation. This is what the Samaritan woman also needed to do.

She says to Jesus, "Sir, I perceive that You are a prophet. Our fathers worshiped in this mountain, and you people say that in Jerusalem is the place where men ought to worship" (John 4:19–20). She was realizing there was something very different about this Man who had drawn her into conversation. How could He know so much about her? She had never met Him. He had never met any of her family members. His direct knowledge of her and ability to articulate her history must have left her reeling with many thoughts and questions. He must be a prophet. It was the only way to explain His knowledge of her.

Bringing up the subject of prophecy did two things for the Samaritan woman:

- It deflected attention off herself and her sin.
- It potentially could settle the long-standing dispute between the Jews and the Samaritans. *Who was right about where to worship?* she must have thought. If any man could set the record straight, Jesus was that man!

I believe she genuinely wanted to know the correct place of worship. I believe she wanted to abandon her immoral life but didn't know how. I believe she wanted a new life, free from failed marriages. I believe she saw in Jesus a path forward to experience that new life.

Jesus knew what was in the Samaritan woman's heart (John 2:25). Moreover, He knew what He was going to reveal about Himself (John 4:26). He did not attempt to keep the spotlight on her sin. He led the conversation so that His divine purpose and will would occur. Jesus is not only a gift of God, Jesus is God! He told His disciples that He had to go through Samaria but didn't tell them why (John 4:4). Something powerful and eternal was going to happen that day (John 4:39, 42):

> Jesus said to her, "Woman, believe Me, an hour is coming when neither in this mountain nor in Jerusalem will you worship the Father. You worship what you do not know; we worship what we know, for salvation is from the Jews. But an hour is coming and now is, when the true worshipers will worship the Father in spirit and truth; for such people the Father seeks to be his worshipers. God is spirit, and those who worship Him must worship in spirit and truth." (John 4:21–24)

Jesus used the subject of worship to help till the ground of the Samaritan woman's faithless heart so that, when He revealed that He was the Messiah, she could receive it. First, Jesus explained that the place of worship should not be the focus. The focus should be on who and how you worship. Next, He stated that true knowledge leads to true worship. Lastly, He informed her that those who worship the Father in spirit and truth are His true worshipers.

Spirit and truth worship is the only worship God accepts. To worship God *in spirit* means to worship from a pure and clean heart. As I stated in the Introduction, God has to give us a new heart and a new spirit. He does this by removing our stony heart and replacing it with a heart of flesh. He then causes us to walk in His statutes and observe His ordinances (Ezek 36:26).

This is what He did with Lydia. Remember Lydia? She was "from the city of Thyatira, a seller of purple fabrics, a worshiper of God" (Acts 16:14). She worshiped God according to the Old Testament law. Since Jesus fulfilled the law (Matt 5:17), God had to open "her heart to respond to the things spoken by Paul" (Acts 16:14), so that her worship was acceptable to Him.

To worship God *in truth* means that our worship must be informed by the Word of God. It means that our worship must be rooted in sound, biblical teaching. To worship devoid of truth means that you open yourself up to deception and easily buy into false worship.

A willfully ignorant Christian is of little use to God. A willfully ignorant Christian cannot worship God in an acceptable manner to Him. This is one reason Christians are exhorted to "be diligent to present yourself approved to God as a workman who does not need to be ashamed, accurately handling the word of truth" (2 Tim 2:15).

Willfully ignorant Christians could be the ones Paul was referring to when he said, "For the time will come when they will not endure sound doctrine, but wanting to have their ears tickled, they will accumulate for themselves teachers in accordance with their own desires" (2 Tim 4:3). Like the Bereans, we must receive the word with "great eagerness" (Acts 17:11), and our worship should reflect that, as well.

Now consider what the Samaritan woman says next: "I know that Messiah is coming (He who is called Christ); when that One comes, He will declare all things to us" (John 4:2). Her response evidenced that the Holy Spirit was working in her heart. She mentioned that she was aware of the Messiah. She knew that He was coming. She knew that He would "declare all things" (John 4:25).

What she did not know was that the Man who had pulled her into conversation, who needed water but had no bucket, who disclosed intimate knowledge about her life, was in fact the Messiah (John 4:26). No one could have prepared her for what she was about to hear, but God!: "Jesus said to her, 'I who speak to you am He'" (John 4:26).

How breathtaking those words must have been. I can imagine woman's facial expression being one of complete shock. I can imagine her heart beating a little faster as the full weight of that statement was realized. As John MacArthur points out, "The fact that He declared Himself so plainly is proof positive that the tiny germ of hope that had her looking for the Messiah in the first place was either about to develop into authentic, full-fledged faith or else it already had sprouted. Jesus would not have committed Himself to an unbeliever (John 2:24)."[3] Without hesitation, the woman left her water pot and went into the city and said to the men, "Come, see a man who told me all the things that I have done; this is not the Christ, is it?" (John 4:28–29).

Just like that, the Samaritan woman was a transformed woman. Her spiritual status had been transformed. Even her social status had greatly improved. Before meeting Christ, sin had separated her from her community. But the gospel unites people. When she left to go into town, she was not the same woman who had come to the well earlier. Her approach to her neighbors had changed. Rather than attempting to stay away from people, she went towards people to tell them the good news. She'd had an encounter with the Messiah.

Although she was in the company of men once again, this time, it was to testify about Christ. "From that city many of the Samaritans believed in Him because of the word of the woman" (John 4:39). When salvation occurs, your heart has been so radically altered that you want others to know what has happened in your life. You want others to experience what you have.

The Samaritan did not hesitate to put the water-drawing aside to do what was far more important, needful, and eternal. Her life was forever changed. She immediately had a new mission in life. She would no longer live for herself. She had meaning and purpose in life. Her life would now be characterized by Christ and His Word. This is foundational to what it means to be a transformed woman of God.

---

[3] John MacArthur, *Twelve Extraordinary Women* (Nashville: Thomas Nelson, 2005), 150.

Dear Sis

When God comes into your life, He takes over your life. He changes you. When God comes into your life, your purpose changes, your loyalty and allegiance changes. You desire to hear and know His Word because You want to live according to it. You desire to fellowship with other brothers and sisters in Christ. Over time, you grow in your understanding of who God is. Over time, you begin to love the things He loves and hate the things He hates. While you cannot attain sinless perfection here on earth, you notice a decrease in sinfulness and an increase in bearing fruit. Your ultimate desire is to live each day for the glory of God (1 Cor 10:31; 2 Cor 5:17; Gal 2:20).

The change that takes place in your life and the maturing of your faith evidence God at work in your heart. We participate in that work according to the Apostle Paul who said, "Work out your salvation with fear and trembling; for it is God who is at work in you, both to will and to work for His good pleasure" (Phil 2:12–13).

Another part of that work is examination. We are commanded to examine ourselves according to 2 Corinthians 13:5 and 2 Peter 1:10, in which both Paul and Peter respectively exhort us as Christians to examine our hearts.

The two charts below are designed to help you begin the process of examining your heart. While far from exhaustive, both charts provide a glimpse into the heart of its possessor.

A heart that has been converted (transformed) by God will exhibit certain character traits, as reflected in the first chart. A heart that has not been converted will exhibit a different set of certain character traits, as reflected in the second chart.

Every transformed woman of God should be growing and maturing in each of the areas listed in the first chart. If your pattern of life is reflected in the second chart, you need to do business with God. Read and meditate on the Scriptures listed. Pray before you begin and, like the psalmist, ask the Lord to "Search me, O God, and know my heart; Try me and know my anxious thoughts; And see if there be any hurtful way in me, And lead me in the everlasting way" (Ps 139:23–24).

Marks of a Converted Heart
Colossians 1:9–12: For this reason also, since the day we heard of it, we have not ceased to pray for you and to ask that you may be *filled with the knowledge of His will* in all spiritual wisdom and understanding, so that you *will walk in a manner worthy of the Lord*, to *please Him* in all respects, *bearing fruit* in every good work and *increasing in the knowledge of God*; *strengthened* with all power, according to His glorious might, for the attaining of all steadfastness and patience; *joyously giving thanks to the Father*, who has qualified us to share in the inheritance of the saints in Light. (emphasis added)

Key Traits		
Isaiah 66:2	**Galatians 5:22–23**	**2 Peter 1:5–7**
Humility	Love	Diligence
Contrite of heart	Joy	Moral excellence
Trembling at the Word	Peace	Knowledge
(moved to repentance)	Patience	Self-control
	Kindness	Perseverance
	Goodness	Godliness
	Faithfulness	Brotherly kindness
	Gentleness	Love
	Self-control	

Marks of an Unconverted Heart
1 John 2:4: "The one who says, 'I have come to know Him,' and *does not keep His commandments*, is a liar, and the truth is not in him" (emphasis added)
1 John 2:9: "The one who says he is in the Light and yet *hates his brother* is in the darkness until now." (emphasis added)
1 John 3:4: "Everyone who *practices sin* practices lawlessness; and sin is lawlessness." (emphasis added)
1 John 3:9–10: "No one who is born of God practices sin, because His seed abides in him and he cannot sin, because he is born of God. By this the children of God and the children of the devil are obvious: anyone who *does not practice righteousness* is not of God, nor the one who *does not love his brother*." (emphasis added)

Key Traits		
Matthew 15:19	**Galatians 5:19–20**	**2 Timothy 3:1–6**
Evil thoughts	Immorality	Ungrateful
Murders	Impurity	Irreconcilable
Adulterates	Strife	Unloving
Slanders	Disputes	A form of godliness
	Dissensions	
	Factions	
	Envying	

What Are Your Thoughts?

1. What stood out to you or caused you to raise an eyebrow in this chapter?

2. What lessons can we learn about sharing our faith with others from how Jesus dealt with the Samaritan woman?

3. What would you say to encourage a woman who thinks her sinful lifestyle is unforgivable? Include Scriptures you would use.

4. How do you think the conversation with Jesus changed the woman?

5. At what point in the dialogue between Jesus and the Samaritan woman do you think her life was transformed?

On a Personal Note

Have you truly repented of your sins and left your past behind? Have you committed your life to the Lord Jesus Christ? If you were to die today, are you confident that you would be "at home with the Lord?" (2 Cor 5:8). How did you come to know the Lord? In a journal, write out your testimony.

CHAPTER 7

Hannah: A Divine Hope
(1 Samuel 1:1–2:10)

> The Lord is my portion says my soul,
> therefore I have hope in Him. The Lord
> is good to those who wait for Him,
> to the person who seeks Him.
>
> Lamentations 3:24–25

The story of Hannah is one of my favorites in the Bible. Hannah's life and legacy clearly point to the fact that she was a true woman of God. Her love for God, her persistence in prayer, and her gentle and quiet spirit all testify to the kind of woman she was. She had an intimacy with God that could not be broken, even in the most tumultuous times of her life.

It's not surprising that the name "Hannah" means grace, and she lived up to that one hundred and ten percent. A more fitting name cannot be found for the woman who became the mother of Samuel, the last judge of Israel. While she wasn't perfect and was far from living in a perfect situation, Hannah was a gracious and godly woman.

All that she was forced to endure for a season would sour and embitter most women. You may know women who are currently dealing with difficult and harsh circumstances. Rather than running towards God, some may be embittered against Him. Rather than responding with a confident hope in God, some may be responding in anger.

Despite disappointment and extreme distress, Hannah did not allow her circumstances to change her attitude towards God nor her actions towards others. Yes, she was troubled in spirit. Yes, her heart was overwhelmed with sadness (1 Samuel 1:8). Yet, as you will see, she did not allow her sadness to alter her character or diminish her love and devotion to God.

The story of Hannah pulls at your heart strings. Like most women, she had a desire for children. She wanted to become a mother. However, unlike most women, she could not conceive. Hannah was barren and was dealing with a lot of hurt and pain because of it.

- **Hannah was dealing with the hurt and pain of polygamy.** Having to share her husband with another woman was ugly, problematic, and disastrous (1 Sam 1:6).

- **Hannah was dealing with the hurt and pain of feeling ostracized and humiliated.** Being barren was a tragedy for women in that culture. It was even viewed as a direct curse from God (Deut 7:13–14). Therefore, she may have seen herself as cursed, and others saw her that way, too.

- **Hannah was dealing with the hurt and pain of relentless taunting, insults, and belittling by her husband's other wife.** Peninnah had an unspecified number of sons and daughters. Yet, she focused her energy on verbally tormenting Hannah regularly (1 Sam 1:7).

- **Hannah was dealing with the hurt and pain of unfulfilled desires.** Year after year, she remained childless (1 Sam 1:7). The unfulfilled desire left her greatly distressed and oppressed in spirit (1 Sam 1:10,15).

- **Hannah was dealing with the hurt and pain of being misunderstood.** Eli, the priest, accused her of being inebriated when she was in deep prayer to the Lord (1 Sam 1:14). Her husband, Elkanah, questioned her love for him and why his treatment of her wasn't satisfying enough to eradicate her longing for children (1 Sam 1:8).

As we begin our study, consider the context. Hannah's story took place during one of the darkest periods in Israel's history (Ruth 1:1). Israel was in desperate need of leadership. At this point in Hannah's life, the last judge over Israel was Samson. You are aware of what happened to him from our previous study in Chapter Three.

No less than four times, the author of Judges states that there was no king in Israel (Judg 17:6; 18:1; 19:1; 21:25). The last time it is mentioned, the author adds the following statement: "Everyone did what was right in his own eyes" (Judg 21:25).

The combination of having no king, no leadership, and everyone deciding for themselves what the right thing to do was, brought about some very unpleasant situations and circumstances in people's lives. Without reading very far into Hannah's story, we are immediately met with the devastating problem of polygamy. I don't know of a worse situation than what Hannah had to endure. The story begins:

> Now there was a certain man from Ramathaim-zophim from the hill country of Ephraim, and his name was Elkanah the son of Jeroham, the son of Elihu, the son of Tohu, the son of Zuph, an Ephraimite. He had two wives: the name of one was Hannah and the name of the other Peninnah; and Peninnah had children, but Hannah had no children. (I Sam 1:1–2)

We are not told why Elkanah had two wives. However, because Hannah's name is mentioned first and Elkanah loved her (1 Sam 1:5), many scholars believe she was his first wife and Peninnah was his second. They also believe that, because Hannah could not have children, Elkanah married Peninnah for posterity reasons. It was extremely important in ancient cultures that the husband's family name continue on and that any land and property belonging to the family remain in the family. Therefore, males born to a second wife had legal claim to the family inheritance.

Note that, while polygamy was allowed by God, it was never His design. From Genesis, God is very clear that His intent was one man and one woman married for one lifetime (Gen 2:22–25; Rom 7:1–2). Multiple women sharing the same man brought sorrow and heartache to both the husband and his wives. Abraham, David, Jacob, and Solomon are just a few of the men whose families were compromised and shattered due to the practice.

Although Elkanah had two wives, he was still a God-fearing man:

> Now this man would go up from his city yearly to worship and to sacrifice to the Lord of hosts of Shiloh. And the two sons of Eli, Hophni and Phinehas, were priests to the Lord there. When the day came that Elkanah sacrificed, he would give portions to Peninnah his wife and to all her sons and her daughters; but to Hannah he would give a double portion, for he loved Hannah, but the Lord had closed her womb. (I Sam 1:3–5)

Elkanah faithfully worshiped and sacrificed to the Lord annually with his family. When peace offerings were made, the one making the offer would roast the sacrificial animal and partake of the feast unto the Lord. The priest would take a portion of it and the rest would be consumed by the family (Lev 7:11–18). Upon returning home, Elkanah gave portions of the feast to Peninnah "and to all her sons and her daughters" (1 Sam 1:4). However, Hannah had Elkanah's heart. He loved her. He demonstrated that love by giving her a double portion of the feast.

The double portion was given deliberately and openly. It was Elkanah's way of showing honor to Hannah. It was his way of publicly stating that she was the most important and most valuable person in the home. This act no doubt frustrated Peninnah. It added more fuel to the flames of her resentment. Perhaps she felt that, if anyone should receive a double portion, it should be her. After all, she had many sons and daughters. She gave Hannah a lot of grief as a result:

> Her rival, however, would provoke her bitterly to irritate her, because the Lord had closed her womb. It happened year after year, as often as she went up to the house of the Lord, she would provoke her; so she wept and would not eat. Then Elkanah her husband said to her, "Hannah, why do you weep and why do you not eat and why is your heart sad? Am I not better to you than ten sons?" (1 Sam 1:6–8)

Hannah suffered greatly over her infertility. She wanted a child. Like Sarah, Rebekah, Rachel, Samson's mother, and Elizabeth the mother of John the Baptist, Hannah felt the constant agony of barrenness. Each of those women were eventually blessed to conceive and give birth.

Unfortunately, Hannah had a house but not a home. The nasty side effects of her husband's bigamous relationship were a constant reminder of that reality. Peninnah was a cruel, heartless woman. Her vicious words and actions left Hannah overwhelmed with sadness, a complete loss of appetite and drowning in tears. It's not hard to imagine that Hannah's day to day life was nearly unbearable.

Peninnah's behavior shouldn't surprise you when you consider she was the woman brought into the family for the sole purpose of filling a void, and it wasn't love. She was the unloved wife, since there is no mention of Elkanah loving her, and she was given a portion of the yearly sacrifice but nothing extra as Hannah was. Scripture spends very little time talking about Peninnah, and for good reason.

It is hard to stomach the fact that some women take joy in another woman's weakened state. Peninnah was that kind of woman. She was jealous and envious of Hannah. Although she could give Elkanah as many children as he wanted, she could not get over the fact that Hannah was the real queen in that house. Elkanah took special care of Hannah and made no secret to everyone of her place in his heart.

It must have infuriated Peninnah knowing that Hannah was valued so highly over her. She took out her fury on Hannah all the more. Nothing was off limits, not even the journey and preparation for worship in Shiloh. In fact, "as often as she went up to the house of the Lord" (1 Sam 1:7), Peninnah wielded the blade of her sharp tongue and cut deeply into Hannah's emotions. If there was ever a tongue "set on fire by hell" (Jas 3:6), it was Peninnah's tongue.

Peninnah was trying to break Hannah, to completely crush her spirit. I can imagine her insinuating that the reason Hannah could not have children was because there was something wrong with her. Perhaps she maliciously told Hannah over and over that she was not worthy to be a mother. Perhaps she insinuated that God Himself had a problem with her and He was denying her children to punish her. This is classic adversarial behavior.

What else does an adversary do?

- They oppose you.
- They are hostile towards you.
- They take pleasure in provoking you.
- They seek to devour you.
- They thrive in disunity.
- They create conflict.
- They attack where it will hurt the most.
- They continually pour salt on an open wound.
- They rejoice over your demise.

Peninnah was Hannah's rival. The word "rival" means adversary. Satan is an adversary to the believer (1 Pet 5:8). Think about it. Elkanah gave a double portion of the sacrifice because he loved Hannah, *but the Lord had closed her womb*. Peninnah provoked and mistreated Hannah *because the Lord had closed her womb* (1 Sam 1:5–6). Satan used the same adversity that God allowed in Hannah's life to brutally attack her and cause her to feel "greatly distressed" (1 Sam 1:10), and he does the same thing to you and me, as well.

A similar situation happened to Job. Remember Job's friends, his so-called "friends"? After losing all of his possessions, his children, his health to a painful and debilitating disease, and even his will to live, Job's friends essentially told him there was something wrong with him. They insinuated that God was punishing him. They blamed him for his suffering. They were nearly crushing his already devastated spirit. They scoffed at him and insisted that he needed to repent. Notice their statements to Job:

- **Bildad:**
  - "If you would seek God and implore the compassion of the Almighty …"
  - "If you are pure and upright, surely now He would rouse Himself for you and restore your righteous estate" (Job 8:5–6).
- **Zophar:**
  - "If you would direct your heart right and spread out your hand to Him …"
  - "If iniquity is in your hand, put it far away, and do not let wickedness dwell in your tents …"
  - "Then, indeed, you could lift up your face without moral defect, and you would be steadfast and not fear" (Job 11:13–15).

- **Eliphaz:**
  - "Yield now and be at peace with Him; thereby good will come to you."
  - "Please receive instruction from His mouth and establish His words in your heart."
  - "If you return to the Almighty, you will be restored; If you remove unrighteousness far from your tent" (Job 22:21–23).

Rather than comforting Job, his friends scolded him. They foolishly inflicted more pain by mocking him (Job 16:20) and insisting that he must have sinned against God. They even implied that because his children sinned, God rightly judged them by taking their life (Job 8:3–4).

In the end, however, God rebuked each of them:

> It came about after the Lord had spoken these words to Job, that the Lord said to Eliphaz the Temanite, "My wrath is kindled against you and against your two friends, because you have not spoken of Me what is right as My servant Job has. Now therefore, take for yourselves seven bulls and seven rams, and go to My servant Job, and offer up a burnt offering for yourselves, and My servant Job will pray for you. For I will accept him so that I may not do with you according to your folly, because you have not spoken of Me what is right, as My servant Job has. (Job 42:7–8)

It's safe to say, putting it mildly, that God has a problem when people speak wrongly about Him, about His Word (2 Tim 4:1–4), and about His people (1 Cor 11:29–30).

The most remarkable part of the entire, horrific ordeal was that Job "did not sin nor did he blame God" (Job 1:22).

Recall from our brief study of Joseph that God allowed him to be sold into slavery by his brothers, which initiated the most severe hardship Joseph had ever experienced. Years later, after remaining faithful to the Lord in spite of his hardship, he told his brothers, "You meant evil against me, but God meant it for good" (Gen 50:20). Satan's ultimate goal was that Joseph would give up on God.

Satan has not changed. He calls into question God's character when you experience times of suffering. He draws suspicion on God's claim of loving you when your prayers go unanswered for long periods of time. His goal remains the same, to get you to despise God, to turn your back on Him, or worse, to curse Him (Job 2:9).

If God is not doing what you think or want Him to do, if He's taking too long to meet your needs, Satan suggests you rid Him from your life. You may be praying for a wayward child, ongoing financial challenges, or failing health of a loved one and it seems God is simply ignoring you. Satan encourages you to leave God out. He continues to ask what he has always asked, *How good can God be if He's leaving you in your trials and hardships to suffer?*

Hannah easily could have resorted to blaming God for closing her womb. She could have despised her husband for marrying another woman. She could have retaliated against Peninnah for her verbal abuse. She could have become a bitter and hateful woman. Yet, she chose humility over hatred. In her darkest hour, Hannah leaned hard and heavy into God. With every ounce and fiber of her being, she clung to God, her Jehovah Jireh.

This is the kind of woman I want to be, and it's one of the reasons I love the story of Hannah. Her heart remained solidly in God's loving care and compassion in spite of the negative circumstances that plagued her life for a time.

> Then Hannah rose after eating and drinking in Shiloh. Now Eli the priest was sitting on the seat by the doorpost of the temple of the Lord. She, greatly distressed, prayed to the Lord and wept bitterly. She made a vow and said, "O

Lord of hosts, if You will indeed look on the affliction of Your maidservant and remember me, and not forget Your maidservant, but will give Your maidservant a son, then I will give him to the Lord all the days of his life, and a razor shall never come on his head." (1 Sam 1:9–11)

Apparently, Hannah's appetite was restored after her husband spoke to her, as the Scripture states that Hannah went to pray "after eating and drinking in Shiloh" (1 Sam 1:9). We are not told in Scripture how many years Hannah was barren. We are also not told how many times she prayed to God for a son. She ate and then proceeded to do what she did often: pray!

Hannah's prayer tells us several things about her and her relationship with the Lord. For one, she knew that God was all-powerful. "O Lord of hosts" is a direct acknowledgement of the sheer power of God. She also recognized God as a general of an army. He was her Jehovah Nissi, the One who could go to battle on her behalf. And she knew that nothing was too hard for Him (Jer 32:17, 27).

Hannah also knew who she was. Her heart posture towards God was made very clear in her referring to herself in the most humble way. She saw herself as a "maidservant," which simply means "female slave." She knew she was a slave of the Lord God, and her desire was that His will be done in her life. Knowing who God is and knowing who I am in light of who He is are two of the most critical concepts in the Christian faith.

In all of her disappointment and distress, Hannah never once accused God of mistreating her. She never once demanded of God that He give her a son. Hannah was the exact opposite of Rachel in her attitude. Rachel would have rather died than continue on childless (Gen 30:1). Hannah was satisfied in being a maidservant to the Lord. She was satisfied in living out God's purpose for her life, even if it did not include children.

Hannah's prayer revealed that she knew that children are a gift of God. Furthermore, she not only wanted a son, but she wanted him to be godly.

Such is the desire of every transformed woman of God, to raise a godly heritage unto the Lord. Hannah's desire for a child was not just about becoming a mother but ultimately about God's glory.

Think about how Hannah began her prayer: "If You will indeed" (1 Sam 1:11). In other words, "If giving me a son would bring glory to You Lord, may it be done." Hannah was not focused on what she could *get from* God but on what she could *give to* God. So committed to God's glory and agenda for her life and the life of her hoped-for son that she vowed to give him back to the Lord all the days of his life. She was ready and willing to dedicate her son to the Lord, vowing that he would be a lifelong Nazirite (Num 6:1–8).

Hannah fervently prayed to the Lord and told Him all that was weighing heavy on her heart. However, I want you to notice what is missing from Hannah's prayer. There is absolutely no mention of Peninnah. Do you find that interesting? Peninnah's name did not come up one time in Hannah's heartfelt petitions to the Lord. She did not ask God to remove Peninnah from her life. She did not ask God to strike her for all the hurt and pain she caused. Peninnah is completely left out of Hannah's prayer.

I am not suggesting that praying for your enemies is unbiblical. In fact, the Bible tells us the exact opposite. We are to love our enemies and pray for those who persecute us (Matt 5:44). I am also not suggesting that prayer for God's intervention in the troubles and trials in your life is unbiblical. Paul implored the Lord three times that He would take away the thorn in his flesh (2 Cor 12:7).

What I am saying is that there are lessons to be learned from Hannah's exclusion of her worse enemy from her prayer. For instance, Hannah's focus was not on her own general comfort or happiness; she wasn't praying for a pain-free life. Nor was Hannah focused on seeking retribution for what Peninnah did to her. She knew that God sees everything. She knew that God was well aware of Peninnah's abusive words and actions. She knew that He would deal with Peninnah in His time and in His own way. Her heart was solely fixed on being gifted a son to the point that she left her enemy's fate completely in the hands of God. "'Vengeance is Mine, I will repay,' says the Lord" (Rom 12:19). Do you believe that?

Unfortunately, Hannah's intense prayer was interrupted with a false accusation and an unwarranted rebuke. To our dismay, Eli, the incompetent priest, could not tell the difference between a woman intoxicated with wine and a woman pouring out her soul to God in prayer. Apparently, he had never seen a woman in passionate, fervent prayer before. His gross lack of discernment is stunning. What an utter embarrassment.

Of all the characters in the story of Hannah, Eli is the most disappointing. He was both a priest and one of the last judges of Israel (1 Sam 4:18) and so was presumed to have a wealth of understanding and knowledge of God's law. He also had years of experience in observing and dealing with people. So, the fact that he thought the worst of Hannah is shameful.

Clearly, Eli was a weak leader, and you don't have to look further than his own family to realize it. Eli's sons, Hophni and Phinehas, were also priests at the temple in Shiloh (1 Sam 1:3), but they were worthless men who did not know the Lord. When the people gathered annually to sacrifice to the Lord, Hophni and Phinehas took more of the sacrifice than their allotted portion as priests. This showed that they despised the offerings of the Lord, not to mention that they were well known to have slept with the women who served at the temple (1 Sam 2:12–17, 22–25). Eli did virtually nothing to stop his own two sons' blatant sinfulness. They both died in battle against the Philistines.

Moreover, when you think of Hannah entering the sanctity of the temple to pray, you would expect sympathy, understanding, and encouragement on the part of the attending priest. While Eli eventually blessed Hannah, it wasn't before adding more hurt and pain to her sorrowful heart. I am almost certain Hannah was not expecting to have to defend her manner of prayer to a priest, of all people. She must have been completely shocked by his ridiculous accusation. Ever the gracious woman that she was, though, even Hannah's protest was offered in kindness. Her humility of heart was on full display as she explained to the elderly and jaded priest that she:

- was a woman oppressed in spirit
- was not drunk wine or strong drink
- was not a worthless woman
- was praying out of great concern and provocation (1 Sam 1:15)

Hannah was cordial. She was polite. She did not lose respect for Eli. Instead, she honored him by saying, "Let your maidservant find favor in your sight" (1 Sam 1:18). She still wanted his blessing despite his ill-founded rebuke.

A Gentle and Quiet Spirit

The way Hannah navigated the trials and adversity in her life was the direct result of maintaining a meek and quiet spirit. Without it, Hannah would have been a very different kind of woman, with a very different story.

Hannah had numerous opportunities to respond in anger and frustration to the excruciating pain and suffering in her life. But she did not! She maintained a meekness and quietness of spirit that makes her stand out as one of the godliest women in Scripture.

The entrance of trials in our lives often exposes the fact that we struggle maintaining a gentle and quiet spirit, bringing to the surface those aspects of our character that reflect sinful emotions rather than a controlled, tranquil attitude. Fear and anger, suspicion and doubts invade our heart and dominate the way we respond to difficult circumstances.

Trials and adversity are that part of life we would like to avoid at all costs. Even though the Bible talks extensively about them and their purpose in our life, we would opt out if given the choice. But Scripture tells us that trials are inevitable and are also ordained by God according to John 16:33.

In God's sovereign plan, He has incorporated trials into our lives (Jas 1:2–4). They have been woven in. They are necessary and a part of His work in producing spiritual growth and maturity in us. While trials in and of themselves do not produce growth, our response to the trial does.

When adversity strikes in life, our first question is usually not *How can I maintain a meek and quiet spirit in this situation?* Our first question is usually, *Why is this happening to me?* or *What am I doing wrong to deserve this?* But Hannah never once second-guessed God about the hardship she faced. While the Bible teaches that all Christians are to be gentle (Gal 5:23), Peter gave women a special mandate. We are to adorn ourselves with the imperishable quality of a gentle and quiet spirit according to 1 Peter 3:3–4.

God has placed particular value and worth on the display of gentleness in a woman's life. Responding to difficult circumstances with meekness demonstrates that we are not overcome by the trial but rather enables us to view trials as "light and momentary" (2 Cor 4:17). It enables us to put our "hope in God" (Pss 42–43).

Gentleness also reflects the character of Christ. When Jesus was reviled, He did not revile back (1 Pet 2:23). When He became angry, He did not sin in His anger (Matt 21:12–13).

A gentle and quiet spirit is the result of fostering a heart attitude that willingly accepts whatever God allows in our life. It is a settled recognition that God cannot make a mistake because His ways are perfect (Ps 18:30). Moreover, it is refusing to blame, question, or become angry with God over His working in our life through adversity.

Unbiblical Perspectives

One of the reasons we struggle with maintaining meekness in adversity is because we view the hardship in unbiblical ways. If what we think about the trial and what we tell ourselves about God is not true, it will be impossible to maintain a gentle and quiet spirit. For instance, some of us believe:

The Lie: *Trials are God's way of getting back at me for my sinful behavior.*

The Truth: God "has not dealt with us according to our sins, nor rewarded us according to our iniquities. For as high as the heavens are above the earth, so great is His lovingkindness toward those who fear Him" (Ps 103:10–11).

The Lie: *If God is good, He will not let His children suffer in adversity.*

The Truth: "My son, do not reject the discipline of the Lord or loathe His reproof. For whom the Lord loves He reproves. Even as a father corrects the son in whom he delights" (Prov 3:11–12).

Biblical Perspectives

How are we to view the hardships and difficulties of life? We must know and believe that:

- **God has made both prosperity and adversity.** "In the day of prosperity be happy, but in the day of adversity consider—God has made the one as well as the other so that man may not discover anything that will be after him" (Eccl 7:14).
- **No believer is exempt from trials.** "For to you it has been granted for Christ's sake, not only to believe in Him, but also to suffer for His sake, experiencing the same conflict which you saw in me, and now hear to be in me" (Phil 1:29–30).
- **God uses trials and suffering to:**
  - *Draw us closer to Him.* "Therefore let us draw near with confidence to the throne of grace, so that we may receive mercy and find grace to help in time of need" (Heb 4:16).
  - *Conform us to the image of His Son.* "For you have been called for this purpose, since Christ also suffered for you, leaving you

an example for you to follow in His steps" (1 Pet 2:21).
- o **Build character.** "and not only this, but we also exult in our tribulations, knowing that tribulation brings about perseverance; and perseverance, proven character; and proven character, hope" (Rom 5:3–4).
- o **Test our faith.** "Count it all joy, my brethren, when you encounter various trials; knowing that the testing of your faith produces endurance" (Jas 1:2–3).

Gentleness and quietness of spirit correlate with inward joy. When James says, "Count it all joy" (Jas 1:2), do not misunderstand. He is not saying trials and adversity are joyful. He is not commanding that you find joy and pleasure in something terrible or tragic happening in your life. What James is saying is that there's another way you can respond, and that is to choose joy. You do not have to respond in anger, bitterness, frustration, or self-pity.

You can experience inward joy in spite of what may be happening around you and to you. James is saying, as you consider the fact that God is at work in your life, joy should fill your heart. As you consider that God only disciplines His true, legitimate children (Heb 12:5–11), joy should fill your heart. As you consider that God is testing your faith, joy should fill your heart. As your faith is being tested, your ability to endure increases, resulting in maturity in your faith and walk in the Lord.

With all that in mind, then, we can see that Hannah behaved with a gentle and quiet spirit because she was a true child of God. She knew God was at work in her life. She knew that God was good and that He does good (Ps 119:68). She chose joy even if God had chosen not to give her a son. We see this in 1 Samuel 1:18: "So the woman went her way and ate, and her face was no longer sad."

Notice that, at this point in Hannah's life, she was still barren. Nothing had changed about her circumstance. Yet, her countenance, her sadness, was no longer there. She was a transformed woman. She was a woman of joy in spite of her barrenness. And now, look what happens next: "Then they arose early in the morning and worshiped before the Lord, and returned again to their house in Ramah. And Elkanah had relations with Hannah his wife, and the Lord remembered her" (1 Sam 1:19).

Hannah's life was forever changed. God gave her a son, Samuel, who went on to become one of the greatest and godliest leaders in Israel. And then, the Lord visited her again and gave her three more sons and two daughters (1 Sam 2:21).

Dear Sis

Hannah could have fallen into despair and hopelessness. Instead, she remained hopeful while falling on her knees in prayer again and again. Nothing you are currently facing or will face is any match for prayer. This reminds me of the following popular analogy:

> The eagle does not fight the snake on the ground. It picks it up into the sky and changes the battle ground, and then it releases the snake into the sky. The snake has no stamina, no power and no balance in the air. It is useless, weak and vulnerable unlike on the ground where it is powerful, wise and deadly. Take your fight into the spiritual realm by praying, and when you are in the spiritual realm God takes over your battles. Don't fight the enemy in his comfort zone, change the battle grounds like the eagle and let God take charge through your earnest prayer. (Author unknown)

What Are Your Thoughts?

1. What stood out to you or caused you to raise an eyebrow in this chapter?

2. What does Hannah teach you about prayer?

3. What does this story teach you about the character of God?

4. How do you think Hannah's faith was strengthened as her trial was prolonged?

5. How do you think Hannah's life was transformed as a result of the adversity she experienced?

6. Why do you think difficult times make us more aware of our need for God?

7. Read Hannah's prayer of thanksgiving in 1 Samuel 2:1–10. List the attributes of God you find in her prayer. What does she say about God's holiness, His power, His wisdom, and His sovereignty?

On a Personal Note

Jesus told Peter, "Simon, Simon, behold, Satan has demanded permission to sift you like wheat; but I have prayed for you, that your faith may not fail; and you, when once you have turned again, strengthen your brothers" (Luke 22:31–32). When life feels like you are being "sifted like wheat," when your heart is filled with sorrow and uncertainty, do you give up on God? Do you begin to doubt and wonder if God hears you? Do you continue in prayer, until you get an answer? Why or why not?

CHAPTER 8

Esther: A Divine Favor
(Esther 1–10)

> The king's heart is like
> channels of water in
> the hand of the Lord;
> He turns it wherever He wishes.
>
> Proverbs 21:1

Are you ready for drama, action, and suspense that could rival any box office movie? I am talking about the story of Esther. It is like a miniseries on steroids. It has a king, an empire, a villain, and an unlikely hero. It contains lavish partying, lots of drinking, and gorgeous women. It will make you run the gamut of different emotions with moments of humor, suspense, anger, sadness, and joy. There are stunning reversals of fortunes, and there are celebrations that are still observed to this day. It is a story that draws you in and keeps you reading until the end.

The Book of Esther is amazing. It is one of only two of the sixty-six books of the Bible named after a woman. The author is unknown, although many scholars believe it was either Esther's cousin Mordecai or Ezra.

One of the most intriguing characteristics about the Book of Esther is that the name of God is nowhere to be found. Nevertheless, while we may question why His name was left out, His presence is undeniable. God's sovereignty, providence, and faithfulness pervade each and every pivotal point and scene in the story.

Few women in the Bible display the kind of strength of character and resolve that Esther displayed. She was remarkable. Although her story took place in a time and culture far removed from modern America, it still resonates with us today.

The story of Esther unfolds from the pinnacle of power. Persia was the ultimate power in the known world at the time of Esther. The events took place in Susa, the capital city of the Persian Empire (Esth 2:1). Susa was located in what is modern day Iran and was the winter residence of King Xerxes (the Greek form of the name Ahasuerus). His rulership spanned from India to Ethiopia, totaling 127 provinces, which is an area larger than the United States. God's name is not mentioned once in the story, but the king's name is mentioned 175 times.

King Xerxes was powerful and ruled with an iron fist. He was also corrupt, prideful and self-centered, with severe anger problems. He was a godless man who was more reactive than proactive. Whatever he commanded or demanded was carried out without question; no one dared to second-guess him. There were times when he was generous, gracious, and accommodating, and then there were times when he was ruthless and downright vicious. As Alice Matthews writes in *A Woman God Can Lead*:

> He was not a particularly nice person to be around. As a matter of fact, you could not be certain of your own future if you got close to Xerxes and then made one wrong step. He was a capricious tyrant, and his will was absolute. He held the power of life and death with a nod of his head.[1]

---

[1] Alice Mathews, *A Woman God Can Lead* (Grand Rapids: Discovery House Publishers, 1998), 165.

From Partying to Paralyzed with Fear
Read Esther Chapter 1.

The Book of Esther opens with a glimpse of the enormous empire and unimaginable wealth of King Xerxes three years into his reign. At that time, he "gave a banquet for all his princes and attendants, the army officers of Persia and Media, the nobles and the princes of his provinces being in his presence" (Esth 1:3). In other words, everyone who was anyone was invited.

That banquet lasted 180 days! That's six months! Actually, it was more along the lines of a military summit in preparation for Xerxes's upcoming invasion of Greece. Therefore, because the dignitaries had ongoing administrative duties in their particular cities, it is to be understood that not all guests were present at the same time. Of course, the king also used the opportunity to display "the riches of his royal glory and the splendor of his great majesty" (Esth 1:4).

Descriptions of fine linen, marble columns, couches of gold and silver, mother-of-pearl and precious stones reveal that no attention to detail nor expense was spared. Even the "drinks were served in golden vessels of various kinds" (Esth 1:7). The wine was plentiful and could be consumed "according to the desires of each person" (Esth 1:8).

At the conclusion of the six-month-long party, an additional week-long party commenced. It was given for the local men, both the elite and the common working class.

One thing is for certain, the folks in ancient Susa knew how to party and had the stamina to keep it going.

As these kinds of events tend to go, the celebrating and free-for-all drinking took a turn for the worse. The six months and seven days of palace partying was nearing an end, and the highly intoxicated king decided to send his dignitaries and special guests off in a climatic way. He ordered seven of his eunuchs to get his wife, Vashti, "with her royal crown in order to display her beauty" (Esth 1:11). Why he needed seven men to escort her is unclear. Also unclear is what was meant for the queen to "display her beauty."

Knowing that the king's heart was "merry with wine" (Esth 1:10), it is unlikely that this was an ordinary or reasonable request.

In fact, it is very likely that the king wanted to put his wife on display as if she were simply a toy or a sexual plaything. He wanted the drunk and boorish men to be captivated by her beauty. He may have wanted them to burn with passion and desire for what belonged to him. Indeed, just as he had displayed his material riches gained through military conquests, he wanted to display his greatest prized possession, his beautiful wife. It was to be the grand finale of his royal gala.

Meanwhile, Vashti, his beautiful wife, was hosting her own party for all the ladies in the palace. It was probably on a much smaller scale, but, nonetheless, the women were satisfied and enjoying themselves. I can imagine the anticipation of the ladies getting all dolled up for a night out at the king's palace. No kids. No cost. No men. It was for women only. No doubt plenty of food, fun, and girl talk was had!

As the festivities were in full swing, seven Eunuchs interrupted Vashti's party to take her away at the king's command. Oh, but Queen Vashti was not having it. She flat out refused to go. Moreover, she knew, as did everyone else, that it was a breach of Persian etiquette for a woman to enter an area where men were gathered.

The eunuchs returned without Vashti. "Then the king became very angry," the Scripture says, "and his wrath burned within him" (Esth 1:12). It is interesting how quickly the king seemed to sober up. His inflated ego suffered a crushing blow. He was furious. He was embarrassed. He was intoxicated with anger. He probably had never been told "no" before as a king.

Vashti's unprecedented response set in motion an equally unprecedented response from him. King Xerxes immediately turned to his wise men for damage control (Esth 1:13–15), who wasted no time making the domestic problem about themselves and every other married man in Persia. They were becoming paralyzed with fear about how Vashti's behavior would embolden all women in the empire. Apparently, they thought all married men behaved like King Xerxes toward their wives.

The wise men made several assumptions about the women of Persia and Media based on zero facts, such as:

- The women had no character or self-control (v. 17).
- The women were in agreement with the way Vashti handled the King's command (v. 17).
- The women would develop contempt and anger toward their husbands (verse 17).
- The women would replicate Vashti's insubordination (v. 18).
- The women believed that the king's command was reasonable and respectful (v. 18).

The most hilarious assumption was that they believed a signed edict could not only control a woman's heart but also make her do what they wanted her to do. They had settled in their mind that submission and respect would never again be a problem in marriages across the land. It was the law (vv. 20, 22)!

Personal Agendas Meet Divine Providence
Read Esther Chapter 2.

Did you notice that the King Xerxes at the beginning of Chapter 2 was very different from the King Xerxes we saw in Chapter 1? The prideful, lavish party-throwing king at the beginning of the story was now somber and sulking over the need to banish Queen Vashti from the empire. A rash but irrevocable decision, born from impaired judgment, was weighing heavy on his heart. He missed his wife. He was forlorn and remorseful, regretting the severity of her punishment.

Did you also notice how quickly the king's wise men devised a plan to replace Vashti? They could not afford for the king to figure out a way to reinstate his wife, for fear that she would then have opportunity to turn against them. If Vashti could have been restored as queen, she most likely would have had the wise men put to death for their part in her loss of position as queen.

While the wise men pushed their personal agendas on the king, his heart was being manipulated and turned through God's divine providence (Prov 21:1). Their advice "pleased the king," because God had already ordained the process that would lead to Vashti's replacement (Esth 2:4).

Their plan was to gather beautiful young virgins from each of the empire's 127 provinces. This was no small task. When it was all said and done, hundreds if not thousands of young women had been taken from their families and brought to the "citadel of Susa, to the harem, into the custody of Hegai" (Esth 2:3). Hegai was one of the king's eunuchs in charge of the women.

Well into the story, the two main characters are introduced, Mordecai and Esther. Mordecai was a Jew and a Benjamite. His great-grandfather, Kish, was taken into exile when Nebuchadnezzar was king of Persia. The family never returned to Israel but remained in the land of their captivity. His late uncle was Esther's father, so Esther was Mordecai's cousin.

Esther was a young Jewish girl whose parents had died, leaving her orphaned. Although Mordecai was not married, he took on the challenge of single parenting and brought Esther up as his daughter. He was a responsible, caring man. As you will see, he was a man of principle and integrity. He may have also been a judge or held some kind of judicial post.

According to Esther 2:19, Mordecai was sitting at the king's gate, the place where community elders, leading men, and respected citizens settled disputes that were brought to them.[2] The timing of his presence at the gate is an important part of the story. Later we will see that Mordecai was in the

---

[2] Kenneth L. Barker and John R. Kohlenberger III, "The Expositor's Bible Commentary" (Grand Rapids: Zondervan, 1994), p. 732.

right place at the right time and responded in the right way after overhearing a threat on the king's life.

The wise men's detailed plan to find a new queen took an entire year to complete. To prepare them for presentation to the king for one night, the young virgins were to be given "six months with oil of myrrh and six months with spices" as cosmetics (Esth 2:12).

Let's be honest. The idea of spa treatments and beauty pampering for an entire year at no cost sounds wonderful. However, the purpose for it in the case of these young virgins is horrible. It was no fairytale, dress up for a night, rags to riches occasion. The young women were being prepared for sexual relations with the king. It was serious, and it was repulsive. Each young virgin lost her virginity to a man simply trying her out to see if she pleased him enough sexually. It was an egregious abuse of females.

Imagine with me for a moment. You are living in Persia. Armed guards show up at your door, all of a sudden. They have come to take your beautiful daughter(s) by force, because the king needs a wife, and the empire needs a queen. You have no time to prepare (as if you could prepare for something like this) but also no choice but to comply. Your daughter is taken away from you and there is nothing you can do about it.

You may console yourself by thinking, *If my daughter is chosen to be queen, it will be wonderful for her and our family. If she is not chosen, she will be returned to me in a year or so.* After all, only one woman could be crowned queen. Even so, the legal kidnapping of your daughter would still mean you would never see her again. Once the beauty treatments were completed and she had spent a night with the king, she would not be returned to her family but instead be placed in a harem with concubines. Your daughter, for whom you had many hopes and aspirations, would essentially live out the rest of her life as a widow. She would be nothing more than one of King Xerxes's hundreds of women, brought to him whenever he might get the urge to spend the night with her.

When Esther was taken to the citadel, she was told by Mordecai not to disclose her Jewish heritage. There would be little if any chance of becoming queen if it were known within the palace. She followed his command.

Esther was "beautiful of form and face" and had a genteel disposition. She did not go unnoticed. Her character, humility, and obedience to Mordecai garnered favor from the head eunuch. Because of it, she received preferential treatment. She was given her own maids and transferred "to the best place in the harem and found favor in the eyes of all who saw her." Clearly, she was respected among her peers; even her competitors found her likeable (Esth 2:7, 9, 15).

Esther was different. She was intelligent, modest, and graceful. She remained humble throughout the entire ordeal. She knew she had to please the king and stand out from all of the other virgins. She also recognized that Hegai, the chief eunuch, knew the king well, including his preferences. Esther listened attentively and followed Hegai's advice when it was her turn to spend the night with the king.

As difficult as it is for us to read what transpired next, for Esther, it would have been tremendously difficult to endure. What she had to do to prepare herself mentally was likely agonizing. A night with the king of Persia was never on her agenda of things she had hoped to do some day. Anxiety, fear, and distress probably tipped the scale in her mind. Yet, she had to remain calm and composed to impress him enough to be chosen. And she did!

The powerful King Xerxes became weak at the knees when he saw Esther. He was overwhelmingly attracted to her. He was completely captivated by her beauty and charm. He had no desire for any of the other virgins. He wanted Esther. His heart was ignited and soared with passion for her, so much so that he loved her more than all the women, favored her, and showered her with kindness, set the royal crown on her head, made her queen, held a banquet named "Esther's Banquet," made the day a holiday for the province, and gave gifts according to his bounty.

The providence of God reigned over the events happening in Susa that day. An unknown orphaned girl snatched from very humble beginnings was elevated to the highest position a woman could attain in the land. There is no way, humanly speaking, that someone with Esther's modest background could have ever been crowned queen of Persia without God's intervention.

It's important to note that, although she was now made queen of a vast Persian empire, Esther was still Esther. "She had not yet made known her kindred or her people even as Mordecai had commanded her, for Esther did what Mordecai told her as she had done when under his care" (Esth 2:20).

After Esther's crowning, one day while sitting at the king's gate, Mordecai became aware of palace officials' plotting to kill the king. He immediately told Esther, who then informed her husband. After an investigation, the two officials involved were put to death (Esth 2:21). All of the information was recorded in the court documents, in the king's presence. This is the first of several providential events leading to the king's eventual full trust in his new wife's family member, Mordecai. Palace life was going well for the two main characters. Esther was the new queen of Persia and Mordecai was in the good graces of the king.

It would all seem to be the proverbial calm before the storm.

Position, Power, and Payback
Read Esther Chapter 3.

After these things, the king's first order of business was, surprisingly, not to reward Mordecai for saving his life. As a reader, you're expecting some kind of recognition or show of appreciation for Mordecai. Indeed, Mordecai was probably expecting a handsome reward. Although it would eventually come later in the story, the initial lack of it highlights the king's tone-deaf judgment and conspicuous negligence. What King Xerxes rather did was promote a guy named Haman.

Haman was a descendent of the Amalekite king, Agag. The Bible repeats Haman's family heritage four times in the book of Esther because the history of his people was no small matter as it relates to the people of Esther and Mordecai. The Amalekites were wicked and bitter enemies of the Jews (Esth 3:10), God commanded that the Amalekites be completely annihilated under the reign of King Saul. Specifically, God told Saul to kill Amalek and destroy all that he had (1 Sam 15:3, 9). When the Lord told Samuel about Saul's disobedience and particularly that he spared Agag's life, Samuel had to fix it. He called for Agag to be brought to him and then he "hewed Agag to pieces before the Lord at Gilgal (1 Sam 15:10, 32–33).

Fast forward to one of the descendants of the Amalekites now living in Persia and recently promoted in King Xerxes's regime. We don't know why Haman was elevated. We are told only that his new position gave him authority over all the nobles and princes in the empire. His promotion may have also meant that he was now the chief advisor to the king.

Regardless, Haman, the descendent of the wicked King Agag of the Amalekites, was now the highest-ranking Persian official under the king. As such, he was to be honored and respected. The king made sure of it by ordering all royal officials serving at the gate to kneel and pay homage to him.

This order of the king was a problem for Mordecai, and it was one he could not carry out. It was not kneeling before a man that was troublesome. As a court official, he would have knelt before King Xerxes numerous times. The problem was kneeling and showing honor to Haman, a descendent of Agag and an enemy of the Jews. No amount of questioning and warning by his fellow servants changed his mind. He refused to bow (Esth 3:3–4).

When Haman saw Mordecai's lack of respect and learned of his Jewish heritage, his attitude was, essentially, *You refuse to kneel, I will kill you and your people.* He apparently knew the history of his own people and what was done to his ancestors at the hands of King Saul and Samuel. As if their God-ordained slaughter had just occurred, he had nothing but venomous hatred for the Jews. Their annihilation became his top priority.

Being the diabolical and superstitious man that he was, Haman drew lots to determine when the systematic execution of God's people would take place. The lot fell on the twelfth month. He wasted no time meeting with King Xerxes to discuss his plan and get the king's approval. Without disclosing any names, Haman portrayed the "certain people" as disloyal citizens and lawbreakers. He capped off his misrepresentations and lies by pretending to be concerned that "it is not in the king's interest to let them remain" (Esth 3:8). His words were convincing, and Xerxes handed over to Haman his signet ring to signify the granting of full authority to kill the Jews. This marked another moment in the story when a personal slight gets turned into a national edict and thereby moves the narrative in an explosive direction.

As the horrible edict letters were drafted and distributed throughout the provinces, the whole city of Susa was in confusion. Totally unconcerned about what was happening in the city, Haman and King Xerxes "sat down to drink" (Esth 3:15).

Haman was a coldhearted, cruel man. He was godless with a complete lack of remorse or empathy. He was full of himself and wanted everyone to know, especially Mordecai, what he had the power to do. As Dianne Tidball states in *Esther, A True First Lady*,

> There was no justification for his actions, the punishment far outweighed the original offence. To slaughter a whole nation for one person's offence is a terrible evil and injustice—the action of a person whose conscience has been so dulled and so perverted that he has no grasp of right or wrong.[3]

---

[3] Dianne Tidball, *Esther, A True First Lady* (Ross-shire, Scotland: Christian Focus Publications, 2001), 66.

Haman represented everything God abhors:

> There are six things which the Lord hates, yes, seven which are an abomination to Him. Haughty eyes, a lying tongue, and hands that shed innocent blood, a heart that devises wicked plans, feet that run rapidly to evil, a false witness who utters lies, and one who spreads strife among brothers. (Prov 6:16–19)

Sometimes in God's plan, He allows His people to fall into very tough circumstances. Sometimes, He keeps us in it and offers His grace as we go all the way through it (2 Cor 12:7–10). Other times, He dramatically rescues us in the midst of it so that there is no doubt in our mind that He showed up and overruled the circumstance (Ps 109:26–27). In the next two chapters of Esther, we will see how Haman's personal agenda was met head-on by divine providence.

Pray First and Then Prepare
Read Esther Chapters 4 and 5.

Mordecai had no way of knowing the level of revenge Haman would extract for his lack of respect. I cannot imagine the horror, grief, and sorrow that gripped him as he read the edict. I cannot imagine the feelings of fear, anger, and despair that filled his heart. Knowing his refusal to kneel to Haman had become a death sentence for him and his people was undoubtedly terrifying and distressing.

Mordecai dressed himself in sackcloth and ashes. He left his home wailing through the streets of Susa until he reached the king's gate. Since the whole city was "in confusion," Jews and Persians alike were all doing the same thing.

When Esther was made aware of her cousin's behavior, she was understandably alarmed. She provided clothes for him to change his outward appearance. His rejection of the clothes set her emotions on edge all the more. She then sent her husband's eunuch to talk to her cousin. What she found out from him must have sent shock waves through her soul. She had been completely sheltered and insulated from matters pertaining to the public.

Esther listened to the details of the agreement Haman made with the king. Note that she neither questioned nor objected to Mordecai's claims about Haman, which reveals that she knew exactly the kind of man he was. And now, because of him, her people were going to be wiped off the face of the earth, and Esther had no idea what she could do about it.

Thankfully, Mordecai knew what needed to be done. He assumed his fatherly role with Esther and instructed her "to go into the king to implore his favor and plead with him for her people" (Esther 4:8).

The back and forth between Esther and Mordecai would sound something like this in today's vernacular:

> **Esther:** "If I go see the king without him asking for me, he could kill me, and probably will. I haven't been with the man in thirty days! You can't ask me to do that!" (cf. Esth 4:11)
>
> **Mordecai:** "I'm not asking! Our people aren't asking! You can refuse, just know that we will be saved another way. And you and your father's family will be executed. I'm very serious!" (cf. Esth 4:14)

I don't know if it was the fact that Haman was going to get away with genocide that compelled her. I don't know if Mordecai's now famous words, "And who knows whether you have not attained royalty for such a time as this," gripped her deep in her spirit. I don't know if it was the fact that Mordecai was a father to her, and she didn't want to disappoint him. Whatever it was, Esther was now willing to do something of great significance at a high risk to save her people. The *I can't* Esther was transformed into the *I will* Esther.

Nevertheless, she waited three days after making what was arguably the hardest decision of her life. She essentially said *I will, but not yet.* Her now famous words—"If I perish, I perish"—demonstrated her courageous determination in spite of the life-and-death risk.

For those three days, Esther and all of the Jews, including her maidens, were to go into fasting for her. Although God is not mentioned in the story, it is evident that Esther prayed to Him, since for God's people there was no fasting without prayer. Before she made any attempt to rescue her people, she sought the Lord.

Then, on the third day, with humility and reverence, Esther prepared herself for action. She got dressed in her regal attire and entered "the inner court of the king's palace, in front of the king's room" (Esth 5:1). And there she waited.

When her husband noticed Esther, "she obtained favor in his sight." The king extended his golden scepter towards her, signifying permission for her to approach the royal throne. "What is troubling you, Queen Esther?" he asked. "And what is your request?" (Esth 5:1–3). In her study through the Book of Esther for *Today in the Word* website, in an article titled "Character Transformed," Kelli Worrall makes an interesting observation here:

> This is the first time in the story that she is directly called "Queen Esther"—and it is by the king. She is referred to by name 37 times in the book. Fourteen of those occasions use the royal designation of "Queen," and all but one of those fourteen happen after Esther 5:1. This was a transformational moment for Esther indeed.[4]

---

[4] Kelli Worrall, "Character Transformed," (February 15, 2020). Retrieved from https://www.todayintheword.org/daily-devotional/character-transformed.

King Xerxes was especially curious about what had disturbed Esther for her to appear before him suddenly and uninvited. Perhaps to ease her mind, and certainly because of his great love for her, he offered to give her whatever she wanted, up to half the kingdom. He loved everything about Esther. She was his new wife and he delighted in her. Whether or not he actually meant what he said is unknown. Regardless, her desire was not for a kingdom or half of it. Her desire was for her people to be saved from extinction.

And yet, all she said to him was that she wanted him and Haman to join her for a banquet she had prepared.

When you think about food and sharing a meal with someone, you think about fellowship, laughter, socializing, and togetherness. You may also think about casual and friendly conversation, mutual love and respect. It may be mind-boggling that Esther prepared a meal for the one who had planned the slaughter of her entire race, including herself. It may be mind-boggling that she sat across from him and ate and drank as if nothing were out of the ordinary.

Yet, her calm demeanor, while authentic to her truly humble heart, strategically resulted in Haman feeling at ease around her. The relaxed, positive atmosphere she set at the banquet allowed her to watch and observe him. She got an up close and personal view of how he interacted with her husband, and vice versa. She listened to him talk and may have even hoped that the topic of the mass murders would come up.

The king, knowing well that a banquet was not the real purpose for her abrupt intrusion, asked Esther again what she needed. As a reader, you are expecting her, without any further delay, to take that as an opportunity to tell her husband the main purpose for the visit. You are expecting her to promptly expose Haman for the devil he was. Instead, she hit the pause button again. For whatever reason, Esther still hesitated. Once again, she essentially said, *I will, but not yet.* Instead, she asked for a repeat event. She invited her husband and Haman to a second banquet the following day (Esth 5:7–8).

The culmination and pressure of all that had taken place up to this point undoubtedly was heart-wrenching. Perhaps in that moment, Esther lost courage. Perhaps the timing was simply not right in her mind. Perhaps she wanted one more night to think about and further prepare her strategy. Esther was wise, patient, and in full control of her emotions. She had prayed and fasted and thus was dependent on God, and He was providentially guiding her.

Meanwhile, "Haman went out that day glad and pleased of heart" (Esth 5:9). He was on top of the world. The highest ranking official just had a private dinner with the king and queen. He probably thought he made a profound impression since Esther invited him to another dinner date with the king for the very next day. He may have thought about his elevation in rank and relished in the power he had over others. Yes, Haman was a happy man.

Until he saw Mordecai (Esth 5:9). With one look at Mordecai, Haman's whole demeanor changed. The jubilance he was feeling instantaneously changed to anger. This was the beginning of the end for Haman. His descent to death had begun. Unbeknownst to him, every act he committed and every decision he made from that moment on would mark a point of no return.

The rage that filled Haman's heart led him to call for his wife and friends, apparently to have them console him or cheer him up. Once they were together, he bragged about his wealth. He bragged about his accomplishments and the number of sons he had. Then he gloated about being the only invited guest of the queen and king to a banquet. And yet, after all that boasting, he concluded with a confession that he was still not satisfied with his life because of Mordecai.

Haman's wife and friends earnestly agreed with him, essentially suggesting that he not wait until the month of Adar (recall that he drew lots) but have Mordecai hung on gallows in the morning and then go to the queen's banquet in peace. "And the advice pleased Haman, so he had the wooden gallows made" (Esth 5:14).

If only Haman's so-called "friends" were true friends. If only his wife loved him enough to tell him the truth. They had to have known that Haman was self-aggrandizing, egotistical, and unstable. They had to have realized that being consumed with such hatred would only ultimately lead to his own downfall. They could have confronted Haman about not allowing the actions of one man to have such an effect on him, basically dominating and controlling him. Instead, their words pushed him further in the wrong direction.

Friends are a blessing, and friends are important. Make sure you choose wisely the people you call "friends." Are they true friends? Are they social media friends? Are they "tell you what you want to hear" kind of friends? Or are they willing to tell you the truth, the kind of friends the Bible describes when it says, "A friend loves at all times, and a brother is born for a time of adversity" (Prov 17:17), and "Better is open rebuke than love that is concealed. Faithful are the wounds of a friend, but deceitful are the kisses of an enemy" (Prov 27:5–6).

A Perilous Predicament
Read Esther Chapters 6 and 7.

The gallows were built. All that remained was approval from the king, and Mordecai's death would be a thing of the past. Given his prior track record, Haman had no concern about obtaining the king's permission. He slept soundly that night. He may have even dreamt about Mordecai hanging from the gallows. He most likely had a pep in his step as he made his way to the king's court early the next morning.

King Xerxes, on the other hand, had a bad night. He tossed and turned and could not get any sleep. Because of his insomnia, he had one of his officials retrieve the royal records and read them to him. It was as if the book randomly opened to the account of when Mordecai was instrumental in saving the king's life. Upon noticing that absolutely nothing was done to reward Mordecai, the king set out to correct his oversight.

Haman, having just entered the outer court, arrived at the right time to be summoned into the king's presence. Without the customary and formal greetings, King Xerxes asked Haman for his opinion on how to show honor to someone. Because Haman was so self-absorbed and arrogant, he assumed the question was about him.

This is classic pride. It's blinding. It keeps us from seeing the obvious because it always causes us to think only of ourselves. As Galatians 6:3 says, "For if anyone thinks he is something when he is nothing, he deceives himself." Ultimately, it sets its possessor up for a catastrophic fall. "Pride goes before destruction, and a haughty spirit before stumbling," warns Proverbs 16:18.

As Haman rattled off all the ways he wanted to be honored, his level of arrogance is staggering. A robe worn by the king, a horse ridden by the king, and basically a parade around the city is about as flashy and attention-grabbing as you can get. As he spoke to the king, no doubt images of the adoring crowds waving and saluting him were vivid in his mind. His vain heart exposed his insatiable desire for attention and glory. One thing was clear: Haman longed to be recognized as a king.

But no sooner did the words roll off Haman's tongue that his swollen spirit got the jolt of a lifetime. His feelings took a sharp nosedive as the king ordered him to "do so for Mordecai the Jew" (Esth 6:10).

The whole scene is one of the most comical parts of the story. It clearly supports the idea that God has a sense of humor.

Maybe Haman's puffed-up attitude pummeled so low that he got a dose of humility for once in his life. If he did, it did not last long. Humiliated, Haman "hurried home, mourning with his head covered" (Esth 6:12). Once again, he gathered his friends and wife around him and whined even more. It would be the last time he complained or even spoke to them. His wife's warning at this point, about not being able to destroy Mordecai because of his Jewish heritage, came way too late. "While they were still talking with him, the king's eunuchs arrived" to take him to Esther's banquet (Esth 6:13–14).

At the close of the meal, King Xerxes asked the same question of Esther that he asked her the day before, about the real purpose for her unexpected visit. For Esther, the time had come to do what she agreed with Mordecai to do, what she had prayed about and prepared herself to do. The moment of truth was upon her.

When she responded to her husband, she was composed, respectful, and did not presume a favorable outcome would occur. She had been with the Lord, and it was obvious. The way she answered him was nothing short of brilliant and brave. She did not know how Xerxes would respond. She did not know if he felt the same way about the Jews as Haman felt. So, rather than begin with exposing Haman, she instead presented her petition as a life-threatening situation, because it was! She wanted her husband to know first and foremost that his beloved wife's life—her very own life—was in danger. After which, she revealed her identity as a Jew and used the word "sold" to characterize what had happened to her and her people. The word "sold" conveyed to Xerxes that money was offered as part of the deal.

It's not hard to imagine the king having a stunned look on his face as he listened to his wife's petition. Her words must have been crushing to him, as he was totally unaware of the threat on her life.

King Xerxes responded exactly the way we would expect. He wanted to know who and where the accused was. When she exposed Haman as the one, she used three different words to describe him: a *foe*, an *enemy*, and *wicked*. These words have similar meaning but with a slightly different connotation. Used together as Esther did, they offered a chilling picture of a disturbed and destructive man:

- *Foe* is the idea of an opponent or an opposing person. Haman was not an ally to the king.

- *Enemy* is the idea of someone who is hostile and bears ill-will towards you. Haman was driven by hate.
- *Wicked* is the idea of someone who is morally bad or evil. Haman had no conscience.

We are not told why Esther used three different words that were similar in meaning. Perhaps she wanted her husband to take a good, hard look at the man he had elevated to the highest position in the empire, short of the king's throne. If he could coerce Xerxes into drawing up an edict to take out a whole race of people, what would stop him from an attempt on the king's life?

Xerxes's heart may have been pounding in his chest as he realized that he had been deceived and manipulated by his closest official, not to mention that he had unknowingly agreed to the murder of his own beloved wife. Astonished, angered, and unable to speak, he abruptly left the room.

Haman, who just twenty-four hours earlier was beaming with self-important joy, was now terrified and begging Esther for his life. His foolish decision to speak to her in that manner would be the last decision he would ever make. It marked the final stretch of his descent to death.

Right at that moment, King Xerxes walked back in the room. He saw what apparently looked to him like an attack on his wife. As he spoke, the anger and tone of his voice was a signal to his servants to take quick action. They had heard that tone before, so they knew what was expected of them. So, "As the word went out of the king's mouth, they immediately covered Haman's face" (Esth 7:8). One of the eunuchs was aware of the gallows Haman had built for Mordecai and informed the king. Haman was hung on the very gallows he had erected to take the life of Mordecai (Esth 7:9–10).

The Powerless Prevailed
Read Esther Chapters 8 through 10.

As the enemy of the Jews was hung, the king's anger subsided. He gave Haman's estate to Esther and the signet ring to Mordecai, who had now been appointed executor of the estate. *The Expositor's Bible Commentary* states that Haman's wealth, title, and power now belonged to his enemy Mordecai.[5]

But the danger for the Jews was not over. With all the good fortunes that had occurred, Esther and Mordecai and all their people were still under a death sentence. The death of Haman did not erase the edict for the mass killings that were still set to occur as scheduled.

Esther, knowing her people were not any better off than they were the day before, unexpectedly went before the king a second time. In tears, she pleaded with her husband to intervene and prevent the massacre from happening. Unfortunately, the king could not fulfill her request as stated. The most powerful man in the empire was powerless when faced with overturning a decree. It could not be done. He knew that once an edict had been written in the laws of Persia and Media, it could not be repealed. The Medo-Persian law was unchangeable (Esth 1:19; Dan 6:8).

By God's continued providence, however, although the king could not rescind a decree, he could authorize a counter-decree. He gave Mordecai permission to write the decree as he felt necessary. It was scripted in such a way that ensured the Jews had the right and authority to defend themselves against any assault on them or their loved ones. The people were certainly encouraged and felt a sense of empowerment as their plight was beginning to change. Mordecai must have been extremely pleased with the reversal of fortune as it was unfolding rapidly before him. The king had elevated him to second in command, and "his fame spread through all the provinces" (Esth 9:4).

When the scheduled day of destruction arrived, the Jews were ready and assembled in their cities and provinces. They had the full support of the king on their behalf. Besides being able to protect themselves, they had something else working in their favor. Many people of other nationalities

---

[5] Barker and Kohlenberger, *Expositor's Bible Commentary*, 738.

became Jews out of fear of the Jews. It gave them an automatic advantage. At the citadel of Susa alone, five hundred men were killed, including the ten sons of Haman (Esth 9:6–10).

King Xerxes informed Queen Esther of what happened. He then gave her an opportunity to make another request and promised it would be granted. Her reply is difficult to understand.

The Bible gives no explanation as to why Esther asked for a second day of bloodshed. It gives no reason why she wanted the dead bodies of Haman's ten sons strung up on gallows. Until now, she has been more or less the perfect heroine. Was she being vindictive? Was she trying to send a strong warning to others who might plan future attacks on the Jews? Did she go too far with her request? The answers to these questions are not given.

The story ends with the two main characters establishing the days of feasting known as Purim. By Esther's command, the customs for Purim were set forth. *Purim* comes from an Assyrian word meaning "lot." It was the lot that Haman used in order to set the date for his planned atrocity against God's people. The Feast of Purim commemorates their victory and his defeat. They were to never forget the day that his evil act was "returned on his own head" (Esther 9:25). It was and still is a Jewish day of triumph, rejoicing and celebration over their enemies.

Dear Sis

Esther did not frantically rush into action. She waited on God. She fasted for three days before pursuing any attempt to rescue her people. Her wisdom, discernment, and listening to sound advice played a huge role in how she moved forward to help her people.

The prophet Isaiah teaches us how we can face the insurmountable challenges that come into our lives. He teaches us the benefits and results of waiting on God: "Those who wait for the Lord will gain new strength; they will mount up with wings like eagles, they will run and not get tired, they will walk and not become weary" (Isa 40:31).

What Are Your Thoughts?

1. What stood out to you or caused you to raise an eyebrow in this chapter?

2. Why do you think "strength" is necessary in facing the challenges of life? Besides Isaiah 40:31, what other Scriptures promise strength to the believer?

3. How does "mount up with wings like eagles" relate to waiting on the Lord?

4. Think about spiritually running a race. What are some things that can make you tired or weary?

5. What lessons did you learn from Esther's life? How will you implement what you have learned?

6. How does the edict regarding women respecting their husbands (Esth 1:20) differ from the command to wives in Ephesians 5:22, 33?

7. You may have heard the saying, "The devil is in the details." In the story of Esther, God was in the details. List as many details in which God's providence was at work in the story.

On a Personal Note

Think about your spiritual life and running the race set before you (Heb 12:1). What are some practical things you can do to keep from becoming tired and weary?

CHAPTER 9

Ruth: A Divine Love
(Ruth 1–4)

> "He who loves father or mother more than Me
> is not worthy of Me. And he who loves son or daughter
> more than Me is not worthy of Me. And he who does not
> take his cross and follow after Me is not worthy of Me.
> He who finds life will lose it, and he who loses his life
> for My sake will find it."
>
> Matthew 10:37–39

Read Ruth Chapter 1

Most, if not all, women are attracted to a good love story. There is something about the romance involved, the exhilarating fun times the couple share and the happily-ever-after ending that we just can't resist.

The Book of Ruth contains a wonderful love story. If you have never read it, you will not be disappointed. Sure, it contains some tragic and sad times like most stories, but the ending will certainly put a smile on your face.

Like Hannah, Ruth lived during the days when the Judges ruled the children of Israel. It was a time marked by turmoil, as God's chosen people repeatedly engaged in a cycle of sin, suffering, repentance, and restoration. This was their way of life, over and over again. It was also a time when "everyone did what was right in his own eyes." That was part of a certain man's decision to take his wife and two sons out of Israel to a foreign land, besides there being a famine.

The man's name was Elimelech. He, his wife Naomi, and their two sons, Mahlon and Chilion, left the Promised Land and went to live in Moab. It obviously seemed right in his eyes to leave Bethlehem, which means "house of bread," for a place where food could be found. What a sad commentary on the negative time of the judges. The "house of bread" could no longer provide bread.

There were several problems with the choice Elimelech made. If you know anything about Moab, you know that it was a desolate place. It was cursed by God because of how it came into existence. The Moabites were descendants of Lot, Abraham's nephew, through an incestuous relationship with his eldest daughter (Gen 19:31–38). She bore a son and named him Moab. The Moabite people worshiped numerous gods and the primary one was called Chemosh. Worship of this idol was grotesque. At times it involved human sacrifices, erotic imagery, and lewd conduct (2 Kgs 3:26–27).

Moving his family from the Promised Land in the face of adversity and hardship was not an act of faith on Elimelech's part but rather an act of doubt. Elimelech's name means "God is King." If he truly believed that, he would have stayed in Bethlehem and continued to trust that God would provide for him and his family.

It is disappointing how the very thought of suffering can lead us to justify doing things that are displeasing to God. Abraham, in a similar situation, left the land of promise for Egypt and nearly lost his wife to Pharoah. He lied about who Sarah was out of fear that he would be killed on account of her beauty (Gen 12:10–12).

God had provided His people with a special place to live, which was the Promised Land. Leaving the land of blessing for a foreign land brought no small share of trouble upon Elimelech's family. Elimelech was trying to avoid suffering and potential death, the natural outcome of famine. Still, deciding to move out of Israel, a place where God was worshiped, to a place of idol worship of Chemosh unfortunately resulted in severe suffering.

Although Elimelech likely intended to return after the famine, leaving the Promised Land was in direct violation of God's will according to the Mosaic covenant. Nevertheless, before we criticize and condemn Elimelech for his decision, realize that, under the same kind of circumstances, you and I most likely would have favored doing the exact same thing. When times seem desperate to us, we tend to do almost anything to avert hardship.

Shortly after settling in Moab, Elimelech died, and Naomi was widowed. We are not told how or what caused his death, but it seemed to be tragically sudden and swift. The fact that it was mentioned very early in the account suggests that he did not live long in Moab. So, as you would expect, the family's suffering began at that point.

After Elimelech's death, his sons Mahlon and Chilion married Moabite women. The wrong choice (humanly speaking) of moving into Moab was perpetuated by these marriages. As John MacArthur points out,

> No devout Israelite men would have regarded such a marriage as auspicious. Israelite men were expressly forbidden to marry Canaanite women, lest the men be turned away to other gods (Deuteronomy 7:1–3; 23:3). Common sense suggests that for similar reasons, marriage to a Moabite wasn't deemed appropriate, either.[1]

Naomi, whose name means "pleasantness of Jehovah or my joy," experienced a glimmer of hope in that she still had her two sons and her growing family. She must have welcomed and loved on her two daughters-in-law in spite of where they had been born and raised.

Sadly, within ten short years, Mahlon and Chilion both passed away. Again, we are not told what caused their untimely deaths. The tragic loss of

---

[1] MacArthur, *Twelve Extraordinary Women*, 71.

both of her sons and her husband ten years earlier essentially left Naomi in complete ruin. All three males of her household had been taken from her, and since her sons' marriages produced no children, there was no one to carry on the family name and no one to care of her. Naomi was a widow, with two widowed daughters-in-law, in a foreign land, left to care for themselves. Needless to say, a profound sense of loss, anguish, and despair absorbed any hope Naomi once had.

However, the very next section of Scripture demonstrates that not all hope was lost. We can see God's sovereignty at work as a tremendous harvest had occurred in Naomi's homeland, just when her world was collapsing.

Apparently, word had reached Naomi that God had visited His people, the famine had ended, and food was now available in Israel (Ruth 1:6). As a widow in a foreign land with two other widows, she knew that the chance of them surviving in Moab was grim. The promise of the famine coming to an end not only revived Naomi's hope, but it also gave her the energy and stamina needed for the journey back to Israel, the place of blessing. This is the first time we learn of Naomi making a decision, which was to return home.

As they began the sixty- to seventy-mile journey, Naomi must have still been heartbroken over the fact that her husband and two sons were buried in a foreign land, a land cursed by God. Perhaps she also became convinced that she had somehow incurred God's judgment. She began to recognize the plight of her daughters-in-law and the fact that any further judgment she experienced would be felt by them, as well. Why should they suffer any more than they already had?

Naomi's doubt of being able to provide adequate care for her daughters-in-law may have been the reason she abruptly stopped the journey and began urging them to return to their homes. This was an act of true selfless love. She had to have realized that for her to travel alone at her age would most likely result in further disaster, but she was willing to risk her own safety and peace of mind so that her daughters-in-law could get married and build a family of their own.

The next several verses (Ruth 1:6–14) contain the most heart-wrenching scenes in the story. Naomi released her daughters-in-law back to their families and back to their culture and what was familiar to them. She strongly encouraged them to return to their homes. It was almost guaranteed that they would be able to remarry and carry on with new husbands. She did not want them to feel in any way that they were mistreating her by returning to their family. She gave them a commendation and a blessing. She essentially prayed for them that the Lord would provide and take care of their needs as they had taken care of her sons and her. Then, all three lifted up their voices together and wept! Ruth clung to her mother-in-law.

Clearly, the relationship the three women had built together over ten years was a close one, no doubt especially since it was forged in the shared experience of tragedy, hardship, and loss. They had clung to each other for support and strength in Moab, Naomi as a foreigner and they as wives of foreigners. Now, for the first time, the weight of separation was overwhelming.

Although it was obviously difficult, Naomi was right, humanly speaking. It is one thing to marry a displaced Israelite living in Moab and a totally different thing for a devout Israelite to marry a woman from Moab living in Israel. She was thinking in terms of their best interests long-term.

The two daughters-in-law resisted the separation. They refused to return to their homes. They contended that it would be best for them to go along with Naomi. Their reason isn't given. Maybe it was for safety reasons or in honor of their deceased husbands' memory, or maybe it was out of genuine love and care for their mother-in-law that they wanted to stay with her.

No doubt during their life together in Moab, Naomi had helped them to understand the customs of the Jewish people. She would have taught them how to prepare the Jewish diet. She would have counseled them on the social and domestic laws of her people and why they lived the way they lived. Most importantly, she certainly would have taught them about the God of Israel.

Their relationship was beautifully knitted together, so separating was not going to be easy. Moreover, what was implied when Naomi said, "May the Lord grant that you may find rest, each in the house of her husband," must now be explained, to remove any further resistance.

Naomi was persistent and did not attempt to offer a false hope. She appealed again to her daughters-in-law to return home. She was truly concerned about their welfare and certainly did not want any harm or misfortune to come upon them because they had not fully considered what was at stake. As young widows in that culture, it was imperative that they remarry if they were to have security and provision for their lives. Naomi knew there would be no hope of marriage within her family whatsoever, so she was attempting to remove any remaining thought in their minds that life would be better for them in Israel than in Moab.

Naomi employed plain, clear logic as she declared she was beyond childbearing years. She explained further that even if a miracle were to happen and she bore two more sons, the women would be themselves beyond childbearing years by the time those sons were ready for marriage. That line of argument suggested that Ruth and Orpah were familiar with Levirate marriage.

Levirate marriage served to keep family members secure and family property from diminishing. It was a law established for the protection of women whose husbands had died and no children had been born from the union. The husband's brother was expected to marry his sister-in-law and father children who would inherit the name and the property of the one who had died. As John MacArthur explains, "If the surviving brother refused to fulfill the duty of the goel by marrying his brother's widow, he was treated with contempt by all of society."[2] Naomi wanted Ruth and Orpah to fully

---

[2] Ibid., 79.

understand that there was no path forward resulting in marriage and children if they continued with her. They had to return.

During this exchange, the Book of Ruth gives us a glimpse into how Naomi really felt about all that had taken place. For the first time, we are made aware of how she assessed her sad circumstances. "It is harder for me than for you," she tells Ruth and Orpah (Ruth 1:13), "for the hand of the Lord has gone forth against me." This was more than just a crying out from a woman grieving her loss. Clearly, we see that Naomi had become bitter.

After fleeing from one hardship (the famine) only to find herself in a far worse situation (a widow), she felt hurt by God. She was angry with God. She felt abandoned by God and leveled a full-fledged complaint against Him. Her thoughts about God will become even more clear when she arrives in Bethlehem.

Once again, before we condemn Naomi for criticizing God, think about how you would feel in similar circumstances. Think about how you face adversity and what you have said in your heart about God. I am not condoning Naomi's bitter attitude toward Him; she responded sinfully to the adverse circumstances that started with the loss of her husband and two sons. But as transformed women of God, we have to accept the fact that we are going to experience times of sorrow and deeply painful situations in life. However, our sorrow and hurt must not lead us to sin against God but to embrace His sovereignty and remember His deep love for us. Rather than asking *Why?*, we must ask *What can I learn through this circumstance and how can I glorify God in it?*

The two women's responses to Naomi's plea were completely different. Orpah, whose name means stubborn, listened to her mother-in-law. With tears streaming down her face, she hugged and kissed Naomi for the last time and left to return to Moab. Ruth, on the other hand, whose name means "friend," held on tightly to Naomi. She refused to turn back. She was determined to stay.

Naomi tried yet a third time to appeal to Ruth that she should return. She even used Orpah as an example of the right decision to make given the situation. Ruth's response was serious, strong, and vehement. Yet, it is one of the most touching expressions of commitment in Scripture:

> But Ruth said, "Do not urge me to leave you or turn back from following you; for where you go, I will go, and where you lodge, I will lodge. Your people shall be my people, and your God, my God. Where you die, I will die, and there I will be buried. Thus may the Lord do to me, and worse, if anything but death parts you and me." (Ruth 1:16–17)

At some point in the span of approximately ten years, God had radically transformed Ruth's heart. Her deeply loving response was evidence of that. She had been converted. She had become a true worshiper of the living God. She must have resolved in her heart that there would be no separation.

Although Ruth and Orpah were both impacted by Naomi and the numerous lessons she taught them about God over the years, only Ruth became a believer. Only Ruth desired to pursue the one true God, to learn and know more about Him. Only Ruth was willing to leave all behind and follow the Lord.

Ruth essentially made a three-fold vow to God regarding her commitment to Naomi. First, she committed herself to Naomi as a loving daughter, since she told her basically where you go, lodge and die, I will go (v. 16). Their relationship would be like a close companionship. She vowed to remain with and look after Naomi's needs for the rest of her life.

Second, she renounced her own people and showed she wanted to be counted among the Jewish race when she said, "Your people shall be my people" (v. 16). As much as Ruth loved her parents, family and heritage, she did not love them more than she loved the Lord (Matt 10:37).

Third and most importantly, Ruth renounced her false god when she proclaimed, "Your God shall be my God" (v. 16). She wanted nothing to do with idol worship and emptiness. She wanted to serve the one true and living God of Israel.

The very last words from her mouth were a call for God to execute divine retribution upon her if she failed to fulfill all that she had just vowed: "May the Lord do to me, and worse, if anything but death parts you and me." So serious and certain were her love and commitment to Naomi and to God that she pronounced a curse on herself if she did not live up to it.

Realizing that Ruth's pledge of devotion to God and to her was real, Naomi spoke no further about Ruth's returning to Moab (Ruth 1:18). As the two women continued their journey to Bethlehem, Ruth was right by Naomi's side. An elderly widow traveling alone was unsafe and unwise. The two women traveling together, though still dangerous, was better than traveling alone.

We might expect joy, relief, comfort, and gratitude would fill Naomi's heart because Ruth was with her. However, nothing could be further from the truth. As the townspeople in Bethlehem began to catch a glimpse of the two women approaching from a distance, no small commotion erupted. The folks were all trying to determine if they were looking at their neighbor and friend from just over ten years ago. "Is this Naomi?" (Ruth 1:19)

The difficult journey back to Bethlehem, the weight of life's hardships, and the loss of all the men in her life had certainly taken a toll on Naomi. Her countenance, which served as a window into her heart, clearly revealed the hurt, pain, and anguish that burdened her. And when she opened her mouth, there was no mistaking how she felt about her life. "Do not call me Naomi, call me Mara!" (Ruth 1:20).

The Hebrew word *marah* (or *mara*) means bitter. It was the name given by the Israelites to a body of water they found during their journey with Moses through the wilderness. After being unable to find water for three days, they stumbled upon an oasis, but the water was bitter and therefore not drinkable. They responded by grumbling against Moses and doubting God's faithfulness (Exod 15:22–25).

Naomi used that same word to describe how she felt returning to Israel after losing her husband and two sons. By calling herself Mara, she was allowing bitterness to define her life.

I can imagine there was dead silence among the crowd. I can imagine the people's faces expressed shock and confusion. Meanwhile, Naomi, whose name meant pleasant, was displaying anything but that. Her angry look, her tone, and the absence of a courteous greeting most likely made everyone uncomfortable.

"For the Almighty has dealt very bitterly with me," Naomi continued. "I went out full, but the Lord has brought me back empty. Why do you call me Naomi, since the Lord has witnessed against me, and the Almighty has afflicted me?" (Ruth 1:20–21). In her comments to the people gathered, she blamed God no less than four times for her tragic circumstances. The people had to have been disappointed at what they were hearing and observing. Any outbursts of cheers and joy over Naomi's return were completely squelched by her bitter words and demeanor.

It is interesting that Naomi made no mention of the fact that she and her husband had moved away from God to enter into Moab. It is interesting that she said nothing about Ruth and offered no gratitude for the fact that Ruth wanted to share her life with her.

The people had to have known that something was not quite right with their long-time neighbor and friend. Straight out of a heart wounded by adversity, Naomi's bitterness caused her to misinterpret all that had happened to her. It caused her negative view of God to be exposed. Notice some of the things she revealed about her heart:

- Naomi believed God had positioned Himself to work against her. (v. 13)
- Naomi believed God was actively working towards her demise. (v. 20)
- Naomi believed God had purposely made her life empty. (v. 21)

- Naomi believed her affliction was God's judgment on her life. (v. 21)

Without question, Naomi's life returning to Israel looked very different from when she left compared to just over ten years earlier. Without question, God had allowed tragedy and hardship in her life. However, God was with her the entire time, and through it all, was sovereignly and providentially carrying her and guiding her. In her book, *The Remarkable Women of the Bible,* Elizabeth George reminds us that "God works in our lives through people, events, and circumstances. But we must also note (and agree) that God never means to make us bitter—only to make us better!"[3]

Unbeknownst to Naomi, she and Ruth were about to experience a profound blessing that neither could have imagined. The turnaround began with the providential timing of their return to Israel: "And they came to Bethlehem at the beginning of barley harvest" (Ruth 1:22). If God's blessings were absent in Moab, He was about to open "the windows of heaven" and pour out an amazing blessing for them both (Mal 3:10).

As the end of Chapter 1 leaves the reader hopeful of what is to come, Chapter 2 solidifies that hope.

Read Ruth Chapter 2

Jehovah Jirah means "the Lord will provide," and Ruth 2 is full of God's provision for Naomi and her daughter-in-law. It begins with the introduction of the last major character in the story. His name was Boaz, which means "in him is strength" (Ruth 2:1).

We are told that Boaz was a wealthy relative of Elimelech, although the exact relation is not mentioned. He could have been Elimelech's brother, uncle, or perhaps cousin. He was certainly much older than Ruth, which will become clear later on in the story. In all likelihood, his age was probably

---

[3] Elizabeth George, *The Remarkable Women of the Bible* (Eugene, OR: Harvest House Publishers, 2003), 147.

closer to Naomi's than Ruth's. Also, we will see that Boaz was not just financially wealthy. He possessed the rare combination of material wealth and wealth of character and substance.

The narrative says that Ruth went to a field of corn to glean after the reapers and then "she happened to come to the portion of the field belonging to Boaz" (Ruth 2:3). Some may think that Ruth got lucky or that it was fate that led her to Boaz's field. No, she chose the field. As Christians, we know there's no such thing as luck, chance, random fate, fingers crossed, etc. We believe that God providentially leads and guides us according to His will. Ruth consciously chose the field, but God guided her choice. God always has a plan. Ruth did not know the plan, but she didn't have to.

It's the same for you and me. We don't know all of what God has planned for us in this life, but when we know and obey His Word, the Scriptures, He sovereignly guides us through His plan. As Christians, we know we are to walk by faith and not by sight. But that doesn't mean taking a leap in the dark. Scripture says faith is the "assurance of things hoped for, the conviction of things not seen" (Heb 11:1). The author of Hebrews gives example after example of Old Testament saints who walked by faith based on the promises of God. Their faith walk was predicated on the Word of God.

I cannot tell you how often I've heard women talking about stepping out on faith because they just "feel good" about something they want to do. Taking a leap of faith about a decision just because it feels right to you is not biblical faith. Biblical faith is walking in obedience to the Word of God. It is following the prescription God has outlined in Scripture. It is being satisfied with following His plan for your life. Take notice of what Solomon, the wisest man, said about decision-making and the sovereignty of God:

> Listen to counsel and accept discipline; that you may be wise the rest of your days. Many are the plans in a man's heart, but the counsel of the Lord, it will stand. (Prov 19:20–21)

> Through presumption comes nothing but strife, but with those who receive counsel is wisdom. (Prov 13:10)
>
> Trust in the Lord with all your heart and do not lean on your own understanding. In all your ways acknowledge Him, and He will make your paths straight. (Prov 3:5–6)
>
> The way of a fool is right in his own eyes; but a wise man is he who listens to counsel. (Prov 12:15)
>
> The mind of man plans his way, but the Lord directs his steps. (Prov 16:9)

Matthew Henry, a seventeenth-century minister and writer, describes God's sovereign control of our lives as believers:

> God wisely orders small events; and those that seem altogether conditional serve his own glory and the good of his people. Many a great affair is brought about by a little turn, which seemed ... lucky or accidental to us, but was directed by Providence with design.[4]

It was the preplanned will of God for Ruth to be where she was and to enter the property of Boaz.

From the moment Boaz steps onto the pages of Scripture, we see a man truly characterized by his love for God and love for others (Matthew 22:37–39). He greeted his hired workers respectfully and without any condescension or disdain towards them (Ruth 2:4). He was familiar with and genuinely concerned about their welfare. He apparently had taken time to get to know them, since he recognized a new reaper in his field.

---

[4] Matthew Henry, *Matthew Henry's Commentary on the Whole Bible*, Vol. 2 (Peabody, MA: Hendrickson Publishers, 1991), 204–05.

Ruth caught his attention and he seemed immediately drawn to her. We will see why in just a moment. Even though she was a young, poor, and destitute woman from Moab, Boaz showered her with special favor and grace. Of course, the Mosaic Law stated that hired reapers were not to gather crops from the corners of the field because that was to be left for the poor and foreigners to glean (Lev 23:22). Ruth fit that category, but not only did Boaz make sure she benefitted from that law, but he also extended her additional privileges.

He offered for her to stay in his field to do all her gleaning. That kind gesture alleviated the need for her to search out other fields and the potential dangers of gleaning alone (Ruth 2:22). He also gave her the protection and companionship of his hired workers by encouraging her to stay close to them while working. And when she needed water, he allowed her access just as he had given his own servants. Ruth was treated like a hired worker with the same opportunity to glean, along with the protection of a safe environment (Ruth 2:8–9).

Ruth was a very strong woman. She had real feelings, real struggles, and real weaknesses. She had suffered deep emotional pain and hurt and experienced great loss. She had undoubtedly sacrificed a great deal to remain with Naomi and risk the unknown in Israel. And yet, the blessing of Boaz and his kind gestures may have caused her to realize that the Lord had been guiding her from the moment she acknowledged Him and began to pursue Him.

Ruth knelt before Boaz and asked, "Why?" (Ruth 2:10). She wanted to know why kindness, blessing, and favor were being extended to her, perhaps especially since she was not just a foreigner but a foreigner from a despised country. Ruth did not know she was talking to a relative, nor did she know what Boaz knew about her until he explained all that he had learned. Although Naomi, bitter over her circumstances, may have ignored the benefit she had in Ruth, Boaz had heard of her remarkable love and faithfulness to Naomi.

He was aware of her decision to leave her country. He was aware that she chose to leave her mother and father and all that was familiar to her. He was aware that she had made a pledge to Naomi to follow her and care for her. He was aware of her deep desire for the true and living God. It had all been reported to him. Her kindness and loyalty to Naomi compelled him to pronounce a blessing on her life. He wanted the Lord to reward her thoroughly for all she had sacrificed. Her actions demonstrated to Boaz that she had fully embraced the true God, under whose wings she had come to seek refuge (Ruth 2:12).

God used Boaz to answer his own prayer. He invited Ruth to eat with his workers. He personally served her and made sure she was satisfied. He instructed his workers to purposely leave extra grain for her that she could glean in the field.

When she completed her work for the day, she had gleaned "an ephah of barley" (Ruth 2:14–17). It was over half a bushel of barley and would have weighed in excess of thirty pounds. It would have lasted for many days or be sold for extra money. This was an incredible amount of grain from gleaning. It not only displayed the generosity of Boaz but also the physical strength of Ruth in carrying all of it back to Naomi (Ruth 2:18). And I would add, it displayed God's abundant provision for the two of them.

Needless to say, Naomi was surprised to see all the grain Ruth brought home after only one day of work. For a female gleaner to have gathered so much was unusual; someone had to have helped her. Curious, she asked Ruth, "Where did you glean today?" (Ruth 2:19)

Ruth told her it was Boaz who had been so generous and kind. "May he be blessed of the Lord who has not withdrawn his kindness to the living and to the dead," Naomi responded. "The man is our relative, he is one of our closest relatives." With joy, she pronounced a blessing on Boaz (Ruth 2:20).

We see here the beginnings of a reversal in the heart and life of Naomi. Her response demonstrated that she, too, had begun to recognize the providential hand of God working on their behalf. She was no longer marked by so much bitterness, resentment, and anger. Her hard exterior broke, and perhaps for the first time in a while, she began to live out in practice the meaning of her true name, "pleasant."

I cannot imagine how Ruth must have felt, seeing her mother-in-law's countenance lifted as she rejoiced over the goodness of the Lord. Only the Lord Himself could have orchestrated such an incredible outcome.

According to John MacArthur,

> The Hebrew word translated "one of our close relatives" is *goel*. It is a technical term that means much more than kinsman. The *goel* was a relative who came to the rescue. The word includes the idea of redemption, or deliverance. Usually a prominent male in one's extended family, the *goel* was the official guardian of the family's honor. If the occasion arose, he would be the one to avenge the blood of a murdered relative (Joshua 20:2–9) or buy back family lands sold in times of hardship (Leviticus 25:23–28)."[5]

If a *goel* was eligible to marry, he was expected to marry the widow of his relative who was left without an heir to carry on the family lineage. As stated earlier in the chapter, this process was known as Levirate marriage, which MacArthur describes this way:

> The Old Testament places a great deal of emphasis on the role of the goel. There was a significant redemptive aspect to this person's function. Every kinsman-redeemer was, in effect, a living illustration of the position and work of Christ with respect to His people: He is our true kinsman-redeemer, who becomes our human brother, buys us back

---

[5] MacArthur, *Twelve Extraordinary Women*, 79.

from our bondage to evil, and redeems our lives from death.[6]

Read Ruth Chapter 3

Naomi had no plan in mind when she and Ruth returned to Israel but undoubtedly began to realize the divine plan God had been leading them towards all along. She was concerned about Ruth's wellbeing from the beginning of their journey home, and it was still her concern because she wanted only the best for Ruth. She found it in Boaz.

After considering all that Boaz had done for Ruth and ultimately for her, there was no question in Naomi's mind that he would make a wonderful husband for Ruth. Since he had already shown considerable concern for both of them, and since she could not be sure of the other relative's desire to marry a widow from Moab, Naomi began to devise a plan.

Naomi learned that Boaz would be overseeing the winnowing of his crop that very night. The winnowing process took place at the threshing floor, which would have been shared by a number of farmers. Naomi was familiar with the routine and basic schedule of the farmers and knew the exact time Boaz would be working there. She catered her instructions to Ruth with that in mind:

- **Ruth was to make herself attractive.** Wash, anoint yourself, and put on your best clothes. (v.3)
- **Ruth was to go to the threshing floor and remain inconspicuous.** Do not make yourself known to the man until he has finished eating and drinking. (v. 3)
- **Ruth was to observe the place where he would sleep for the night.** You shall notice the place where he lies. (v. 4)

---

[6] Ibid., 79–80.

- **She was to go into his quarters, expose his feet, and lie down.** You shall go and uncover his feet and lie down; he will tell you what to do. (v. 4)

Naomi concluded her instructions with the words, "He will tell you what you shall do" (Ruth 3:3–4). Ruth was enthralled with her mother-in-law. Her unquestioned obedience evidenced the level of trust she had for her. Of course, it's already obvious that Ruth was also a woman of emotional and physical strength, productive and resourceful, a woman of initiative, discipline, and self-motivation. These qualities combined well with a submissive heart attitude. Ruth willfully listened and submitted to Naomi's advice, responding with "All that you say I will do" (Ruth 3:5). According to the modern feminist, a submissive woman is a weak woman. She is cowardly and allows herself to be dominated by male chauvinism. However, in Ruth we see the biblical combination of strength, submission, and ingenuity with a gentle spirit.

After taking notice of where Boaz slept for the night, Ruth entered, uncovered his feet, and laid down. In the middle of the night, he was startled awake, only to discover a woman lying at his feet. He asked her who she was.

I don't know if Ruth became nervous trying to carry out a bizarre and unfamiliar Jewish custom. I don't know if she, too, was startled and forgot some of what Naomi said. Rather than letting Boaz tell her what she should do, the opposite occurred. She identified herself and immediately told Boaz what to do. "I am Ruth, your maid," she replied. "So, spread your covering over your maid, for you are a close relative" (Ruth 3:9).

Was that a marriage proposal? Did Ruth ask Boaz to marry her? Was she asking him to be her kinsman-redeemer? Thankfully, being the honorable man that he was, Boaz had already demonstrated a willingness to perform the duties of a kinsman-redeemer. In response, he pronounced another blessing on her. First, he praised her. Next, he informed her. Lastly, he reassured her. He praised her for her kindness towards him, saying she could have desired a younger man "whether poor or rich" (Ruth 3:10).

Ruth's response from there made it clear that she had decided to act within the will of God rather than by her own personal motivations. Sure, when you think about it, even for a godly woman, a man closer to her age would have been more appealing than someone Boaz's age. If for no other reason, she had been widowed once and marrying an older man would be opening herself up to the possibility of that happening again. Boaz informed her that there actually was someone closer than him who had the responsibility to fulfill the kinsman-redeemer duties. The Mosaic law was clear that the widow was to marry the closest relative of the deceased. Boaz comforted her and promised that he would marry her if the closer relative refused.

Boaz continued in demonstration of his care and concern for Ruth by instructing her to remain with him until the early morning. To protect her reputation, he had her return at a time "before one could recognize another; and he said, 'Let it not be known that the woman came to the threshing floor'" (Ruth 3:14).

Ruth did not return empty-handed. Boaz gave her six measures of barley. Naomi, who undoubtedly was waiting on pins and needles for her return, must have been beaming with joy as Ruth told her "all that the man had done for her" (Ruth 3:16). Perhaps Naomi may have come under conviction as she was beginning to experience the bountiful blessings the Lord had given her through Boaz. When she and Ruth arrived back in Israel and before Boaz came on the scene, she had made statements about God that were not true. Do you remember what she said? "I went out full, but the Lord has brought me back empty" (Ruth 1:21). She believed God had afflicted and emptied her life, when, in fact, He was in the process of reversing her unfortunate circumstances. All along, God was moving and working to fill her life in His context of blessings, not hers.

Read Ruth Chapter 4.

The end of Chapter 3 concludes with Naomi and Ruth waiting. Both having done all that they could do so far, they waited for the kinsman redeemer situation to be settled. Would Ruth marry Boaz, or would a closer relative be her future husband? Just as Naomi predicted, Boaz would settle the matter that same day.

Chapter 4 begins with Boaz making his way to the city gates. The other relative just happened to be "passing by, so he said, 'Turn aside, friend, sit down here'" (Ruth 4:1). It was yet another example of God providentially controlling life's events. The nearer kinsman had no idea what he was about to encounter, yet God had him at the city gates just in time to meet with Boaz.

The city gate was the place where the elders of the city sat and ruled. Recall from our study in the Book of Esther, these were community leaders who were considered the judge and jury of a city, and whatever they ruled on was law for that particular place. Since both Levirate marriage and property redemption were legal matters, the situation had to be settled before the elders, at the city gates.

As the elders gathered and the meeting began, Boaz explained to the close relative that Naomi was in possession of her late husband's land. She needed to sell the land to help provide for her and her daughter-in-law. Although opportunities to glean would take care of them during harvest season, their long-term survival required additional cash that selling the land would furnish. Boaz carefully crafted his speech without yet disclosing Ruth's connection to the land.

As expected, the nearest kinsman jumped at the opportunity (Ruth 4:2–4). The purchase of the land from Naomi, who had no children nor could have them at this point, would mean that the land would permanently be his inheritance. He could easily take care of Naomi from the proceeds of the land's produce. Both legally and financially, it was a wise choice.

While the nearer kinsman was still smiling and preparing to seal the deal, Boaz continued talking. He informed him of a specific duty that must be carried out related to the sale of the property. "On the day you buy the field from the hand of Naomi," he began, "you must also acquire Ruth the Moabitess, the widow of the deceased, in order to raise up the name of the deceased on his inheritance" (Ruth 4:5).

After hearing this additional detail, the nearest kinsman immediately lost interest in the deal. With Ruth now a factor in the equation, there was the likelihood of children being born who would not only have legal right to the purchased land but also ownership rights to the kinsman's land. He was unwilling to go through with the transaction and thereby relinquished his legal right to the property. This, in turn, opened the door for Boaz to purchase the land from Naomi and marry Ruth. Which he did!

Boaz married Ruth with the full intention of fulfilling his obligation to produce an heir for Mahlon "so that the name of the deceased may not be cut off from his brothers or from the court of his birthplace" (Ruth 4:10).

All of the people observing along with the elders acknowledged that they were witnesses of the transaction and marriage of Boaz to Ruth. The elders then pronounced a blessing on Boaz and Ruth (Ruth 4:11–12), which came to fruition as God removed Ruth's barrenness and she conceived and gave birth to a son. What she was unable to do for ten years married to Mahlon, God enabled her to do now married to Boaz.

At the birth of Ruth's and Boaz's son, the narrative shifts attention to the town's women and to Naomi.

Recall that the women were astonished at Naomi's emotional condition when she first returned to Bethlehem. They saw a woman in despair, who spoke from the depths of her emptiness and discouragement. They heard her speak negatively about God. Now, with the birth of her first grandchild, they saw something very different in her. They saw a satisfied woman, joyful with her life and circumstances. They saw a woman unforsaken by God and filled with His blessings. It compelled them to give praise to the Lord and to speak about His faithfulness to her.

The women wanted Naomi to know that God had not left her without a guardian redeemer. Their desire was that her grandson would become famous in Israel. They were confident that he would both renew and sustain her life even as she grew old. They concluded their encouraging words by reminding her that the greatest blessing the Lord gave her was Ruth, who loved her and was better to her than seven sons.

For Ruth, she had so identified with and was beloved by the town's women that they were given the honor of naming her son. "And they named him Obed. He was the father of Jesse, the father of David" (Ruth 4:17). This is where the Book of Ruth saves the very best for last! It is at the end of the story that we find out God had reserved a special place for Ruth in the genealogy of His Son. Ruth, the Moabitess, who was an outsider from a land cursed by God, was grafted into the royal line of the Messiah. Her son Obed became the father of Jesse, who was the father of David, and Jesus was called the "Son of David." Ruth was not only the great-grandmother of David, but she was also one of only five women specifically named in the lineage of the Lord Jesus Christ. That means that Jesus, the Savior of the world, was also a descendant of Ruth!

Ruth had no way of knowing that her decision to remain with Naomi would result in a rich family heritage. For through her the promised seed that God spoke of in the Garden of Eden would be born.

What an amazing story! What an amazing life!

Dear Sis

"God knows the plans He has for you, plans to prosper and not harm you, plans to give you hope and a future" (Jer 29:11; Rom 8:28). The Lord has established and set forth your life according to His perfect will.

Now, you must do as Ruth did. You must leave behind all that is contrary and in opposition to the will of God. You must determine to follow hard after Him!

Your past does not define you. Your past does not have to be the last chapter of your life. It does not render you useless to God. Although it is part of your life, it should never be the controlling influence in your life. Only you determine the extent and impact that your past will have on your present. Consider these words from Paul:

> Brothers and sisters, I do not consider myself yet to have taken hold of it. But one thing I do: Forgetting what is behind and straining toward what is ahead, I press on toward the goal to win the prize for which God has called me heavenward in Christ Jesus. (Phil 3:13–14)

Sometimes, the best path forward is not necessarily the easiest. Ruth suffered and endured many unpleasant circumstances. Moreover, she chose to leave family and friends and the only culture she had ever known. She left behind all that was familiar to be with a grief-stricken and bitter mother-in-law, who offered little hope of a better life with her. Yet, her mind was set on doing whatever was necessary to lay hold of the true and living God. She never looked back, and she never regretted her decision.

It was not an easy decision. Nevertheless, Ruth obeyed the Lord, regardless of personal pain or loss. She had an intense determination for the things of God, and it was obvious that He favored and prospered her life.

When I think about Ruth and her extraordinary story, I am reminded that we serve a God who redeems and transforms people. I am reminded that we serve a God who has room in His kingdom for people from all ethnicities, nationalities, and cultures. In Ruth's case, he extracted her out of an evil, idolatrous country and made her His own. He chooses whomever and from wherever to be His own. He changes our heart, cleans up our life, and gives us an insatiable desire to please Him.

When I think about the story of Ruth, I am reminded that we serve a God who sits high yet looks low (Ps 138:6). He watches over and providentially orders the very details of our life, resulting in His purpose and will being accomplished.

The following lyrics from one of my favorite songs come to mind when I think about Ruth and how she handled loss, sadness, and uncertainty in her life:

"His Eye Is on the Sparrow"
By Civilla D. Martin and Charles H. Gabriel

Why should I feel discouraged
Why should the shadows come
Why should my heart feel lonely
And long for heaven and home
When Jesus is my portion
A constant friend is He
His eye is on the sparrow
And I know He watches over me.

"Let not your heart be troubled,"
His tender word I hear
And resting on His goodness
I lose my doubts and fears;
Though by the path He leadeth
But one step I may see
His eye is on the sparrow
And I know He watches me.

Whenever I am tempted
Whenever clouds arise

When songs give place to sighing
When hope within me dies
I draw the closer to Him
From care He sets me free
His eye is on the sparrow
And I know He watches me.

What Are Your Thoughts?

1. What stood out to you or caused you to raise an eyebrow in this chapter?

2. Elimelech's decision to move his family to Moab ultimately resulted in severe suffering for Naomi. Can you relate to Naomi? Have you ever felt disappointed or let down by God? Have you ever felt you were being judged by God? How did you overcome those thoughts and set your mind right towards Him?

3. Each of us, like Naomi, has experienced painful circumstances. Have you ever become bitter with life's circumstances? What can you share about how God brought you out of your bitterness?

4. What does Ruth's determination to go with Naomi teach you about hope?

5. At the suggestion of Naomi, Ruth asked Boaz to be her husband. It was a marriage proposal. Is it unbiblical for women to propose to men? Why or why not? Is it wise for a woman to propose to a man? Why or why not? Give biblical support for your answer.

6. What character traits do you see in Ruth and how she handled her circumstance?

7. If you are unmarried, what does Boaz teach you about the kind of man you should be praying for?

8. If you have a son, what does Boaz teach you about training your son for manhood?

On a Personal Note

What do you do to maintain a biblical view of God when experiencing adversity?

CHAPTER 10

The Titus 2 Woman: A Divine Mandate
(Titus 2:3–5)

> Many daughters have done nobly, but you excel them all.
> Charm is deceitful and beauty is vain, but a woman
> who fears the Lord, she shall be praised.
>
> Proverbs 31:29–30

In case you hadn't realized it, we are living in a health-crazed society. We are overwhelmed with choices designed to ensure we live a healthy lifestyle. Whether it's physical health, emotional health, mental health, social health, or financial health, there is something on the market to help you reach your goals. Generally, when we hear the word "health," one or all of these five areas will come to mind. Rarely, if ever, does the church come to mind. Yet, the Bible has a lot to say about the church and its condition, whether healthy or otherwise.

One specific facet of the church that evidences good health, or the lack thereof, is the role of women in Christian service or ministry. We play a huge and vital role in the overall health and wellbeing of the church. Are we ministering the way God established and designed? A church without women functioning in their God-given roles is an unhealthy and ineffective church as God has purposed for the local church to be.

Some of the key roles established for women within the divine community are found in Paul's instruction to Timothy regarding widows. Not all women will be married or bear children. However, for most women, their ministry begins in the home. Notice Paul's specific details here:

> A widow is to be put on the list only if she is not less than sixty years old, having been the wife of one man, having a reputation for good works, and if she has brought up children, if she has shown hospitality to strangers, if she has washed the saints' feet, if she has assisted those in distress, and if she has devoted herself to every good work. (1 Tim 5:9–10)

A church with women who have a reputation for good works, brought up children, shown hospitality, served the saints, assisted those in distress and devoted themselves to every good work, is strong evidence of a healthy church.

However, there is more.

When Paul established the church on the island of Crete, he left Titus there to "set in order what remains and appoint elders in every city" (Titus 1:5). To the congregation of believers, Titus was also to "speak the things which are fitting for sound doctrine" (Titus 1:9; 2:1). Indeed, in the first ten verses of Titus 2, Paul references sound doctrine four different times, and among "the things which are fitting for sound doctrine" are Paul's specific instructions regarding how men and women within a local fellowship should live as the body of Christ.

Since the things spoken by Titus were to be fitting for sound doctrine, it is to be understood that those receiving Titus's teaching desired sound doctrine for themselves. In particular for readers of *Unhinged No More*, older women charged with teaching the younger women in the church must be characterized by sound doctrine. That includes you as well as me.

What is Sound Doctrine?

In its simplest definition, sound doctrine is truth. It is teaching that rightly defines who God is and identifies and declares His works and His will. For example, we have been created by God, in His image and for His glory. Sound doctrine must include how we glorify God as His image bearers. The purpose is to know and love God, resulting in living a life that reflects that knowledge and love.

Sound doctrine

- promotes holy living
- promotes unity with our brothers and sisters in Christ
- promotes God-honoring worship
- safeguards us from false teaching
- gives us confidence in sharing our faith
- enables us to interpret Scripture accurately

Now, let's identify two main virtues of a woman of sound doctrine before we discuss the divine mandate of Titus 2.

Main Virtue One: A woman of sound doctrine knows and believes that the Bible is sufficient.

A woman of sound doctrine is not relying on something outside of Scripture to instruct her. She is not wanting her ears tickled or to learn how to become a better version of herself. She is not looking for "more" for herself except a closer relationship with God for His purpose and glory.

She is not hoping to hear from God or trying to discern His voice outside of Holy Scripture. She eagerly opens His Word and makes it her goal to understand and obey what thus says the Lord. A woman of sound doctrine finds her identity in Scripture and is satisfied with it!

Main Virtue Two: A woman of sound doctrine knows and believes that the Bible is relevant.

A woman of sound doctrine knows that the Bible is as relevant today as it was when it was written, and as it will always be. The Bible is the same yesterday, today, and forever, because the Author of the Bible is the same yesterday, today, and forever. It contains "everything pertaining to life and godliness, through the true knowledge of Him who called us by His own glory and excellence" (2 Pet 1:3).

She knows and believes that the Word of God is "living and active, and sharper than any two-edged sword, even penetrating as far as the division of soul and spirit, of both joints and marrow, and able to judge the thoughts and intentions of the heart" (Heb 4:12).

She knows and believes that the Holy Bible is "inspired by God and profitable for teaching, for reproof, for correction, for training in righteousness; so that the man of God may be adequate, equipped for every good work" (2 Tim 3:16–17).

A woman of sound doctrine does not allow herself to be caught up or "tossed here and there by waves and carried about by every wind of doctrine" (Eph 4:14). She is stable, sober-minded and "understands what the will of the Lord is" (Eph 5:17).

In Paul's pastoral letter to Titus, when he begins instructing Titus specifically regarding women in the church, the first attribute he mentions is "reverent in their behavior" (Titus 2:3). In his work on Christian marriage, my husband, Roger Skepple, explains it this way:

> The word *reverent* is derived from combining two Greek words, temple and fitting or suitable. The word *behavior* means deportment or demeanor. What is being pictured in these two words is a woman who carries and conducts herself much like a priest would in service to God in the temple. She has an internal frame of reference that is regulated by God's standards and not her own. She takes her belonging to God seriously, so much so, that she strives

to correspond every aspect of her conduct and life to God's will."[1]

One of the ways reverent behavior manifests itself in women is in our actions and speech, and Paul gets very specific about this in the rest of verse 3. Firstly, women were not to be enslaved to or drunk with wine, for obvious reasons. Drinking alcohol was not forbidden, just as it is not forbidden today. Rather, the problem is becoming intoxicated or controlled by it, which would render her unfit and useless in teaching and encouraging women in the Lord.

Next, the older women were not to be malicious gossips. This is the second time Paul mentions "malicious gossips" in Scripture in reference to women. The first time is when he gives Timothy the qualifications of a deaconess (1 Tim 3:11). A woman's speech will either disqualify her or affirm her (1 Cor 9:27). Let's examine this principle more closely.

The Ministry of Shut Up

> He who guards his mouth and his tongue, guards his soul
> from troubles. (Prov 21:23)

The heading above may cause you to cringe. The words "shut up" are abrasive and offensive. In fact, in my parent's house, they were considered curse words. My siblings and I were not allowed to say them to each other or there would be unbearable consequences.

I chose that heading after hearing it in a Titus 2 Bible study I attended. It was a creative reminder of the approach we must take when it comes to gossip. Gossip should be viewed much like you would something that has a

---

[1] Roger W. F. Skepple, Sermon from "The Christian Marriage Series" (2000), Atlanta, GA: Berean Bible Baptist Church.

foul or putrid smell to it, something that is repulsive to you. You should want to get away from it as quickly as you can.

What is Gossip?

If gossip were personified—and would be honest about itself—I imagine it would describe itself as Charles Kimball presented it in his sermon, "Gossip: The Eighth Deadly Sin":

> Who am I? I have no respect for justice. I maim without killing. I break hearts and ruin lives. I am cruel and malicious and gather strength with age. The more I am quoted, the more I am believed. I flourish at every level of society. My victims are helpless. They cannot protect themselves against me because I have no name and no face. To track me down is impossible. The harder you try, the more elusive I become. I'm nobody's friend. Once I tarnish a reputation, it is never the same. I topple governments and ruin marriages. I destroy careers and cause heartache and sleepless nights. I wreck churches and separate Christians. I spawn suspicion and generate grief, make innocent people cry on their pillows. Even my name hisses. I am GOSSIP.[2]

Gossip is sin. As with all sin, it begins in the heart. It is born out of a critical spirit and shaped in negativity, antagonism, and a desire to harm. Its goal is to tear down and destroy through shaming others and speaking about them in the most unfavorable way. It is an aggressive desire to slander and spread information about others that you would not speak in their presence.

"Malicious gossips" (v. 3) comes from one Greek word, *diabolos*, which means slanderer. Satan is a slanderer and accuser of the brethren (Rev 12:10).

---

[2] Charles Kimball, "Gossip: The 8th Deadly Sin Proverbs 18:8" (n.d.). Retrieved from https://www.preaching.com/sermons/gossip-the-8th-deadly-sin- proverbs-188

To engage in gossip, by either speaking it or listening to it, is to participate in the devil's work. You become an ally with him when you gossip.

The Bible has a lot to say about gossip. It is no small matter with God. He likens it to murder, malice, and an inventor of evil. Read Romans 1:29–30; Proverbs 4:24; 10:18; 16:28; 20:19; Ephesians 4:29; and James 1:26 to learn specifically how God views gossip. Also consider how the Bible describes sins of the tongue in general. It will give you a whole new perspective on the proverbial "think before you speak."

"Your tongue devises destruction, like a sharp razor, o worker of deceit. You love evil more than good, falsehood more than speaking what is right. You love all words that devour, o deceitful tongue." (Ps 52:2–4)	**Sins of the Tongue** • It devises destruction. • It is like a sharp razor. • It is full of deceit. • It loves evil and falsehood. • It loves words that devour.
"There are six things which the Lord hates, yes, seven which are an abomination to Him. Haughty eyes, a lying tongue, and hands that shed innocent blood, a heart that devises wicked plans, feet that run rapidly to evil, a false witness who utters lies, and one who spreads strife among brothers." (Prov 6:16–19)	**Sins of the Tongue** • It is characterized by lies. • It is a false witness that utters lies. • It spreads strife among brothers.
"And the tongue is a fire, the very world of iniquity, the tongue is set among our members as that which	**Sins of the Tongue** • It is set among our members. • It defiles the entire body.

defiles the entire body, and sets on fire the course of our life and is set on fire by hell.... But no one can tame the tongue; it is a restless evil and full of deadly poison." (Jas 3:6, 8)	• It sets on fire the course of life. • It is set on fire by hell. • It is a restless evil. • It is full of deadly poison.

John MacArthur has said:

> Whereas men tend to be rough and violent in their actions, women have a tendency to be rough and violent in their words. Older women who find themselves with time on their hands can be tempted to allow their conversations to lead to gossip, criticism, and slander.[3]

I am guilty of gossip. Chances are high that you are, too. We have all engaged in gossip at times in our lives. If that's not bad enough, we have friends and acquaintances that gossip. Nonetheless, the Word of God is clear. God hates gossip. And since He hates it, we must hate it also.

God's Word further warns us against the sin of gossip, including the following descriptions, admonitions, and warnings:

- Gossips are usually talkers; a gossip loves to talk. (Prov 10:19)
- Where there is drama, gossip thrives. (2 Cor 12:20)
- Gossip never solves problems. (Prov 26:20)
- A gossip needs an available and willing ear. (Prov 20:19; Exod 23:1)
- Gossip kills:
  - the testimony and/or spiritual witness of the gossiper

---

[3] John MacArthur, *Divine Design* (Colorado Springs: David C. Cook Publishers, 2011), 204.

- fellowship among Believers
- relationships
- reputations
- trust

Gossip must be confronted and confessed, and repentance must be pursued. A transformed woman of God must have an outward behavior that springs from an inward focus upon God. She must resist the pull of her flesh, the patterns of the world and the lures of the devil that tempt her with gossip wherever it tries to rear its ugly head. She must be sharp in her senses, because she has the highly important task of teaching what is good to the younger women in the church.

The Ministry of Speak Up

> She opens her mouth in wisdom and the teaching of kindness is on her tongue. (Prov 31:26)

The last instruction for the older women in the church that Paul identifies in verse three is that we are to teach what is good. Older women in the church are to be teachers of good things. They have learned and experienced the very things the younger women are currently facing. Rather than being idle busybodies "talking about things not proper to mention" (1 Tim 5:13), Paul assigns to them the wonderful, life-changing ministry of teaching younger women what is good.

What young woman who truly loves the Lord and wants to grow in His grace and in the knowledge of Him would deny the help, wisdom, and encouragement that an older woman can offer?

When my children were very young, the Lord put a lady in my life, Julie Pyne, who was just a few years older than me but was nevertheless my "older woman." The practical ways she modeled real womanhood and the commonsense lessons she taught me about being sensible, making a house a home and keeping it, and how to love my husband and children, were an illustration of the Titus 2 mandate. There was no book or set of notes to which she referred. There was no classroom atmosphere or lectern involved. The lessons came about in the day-to-day ebbs and flows of life as we spent time together. She was steadily teaching, and I was watching and learning.

I believe this was the vision Paul had in mind when he told Titus how to organize the church of Crete. Older women should occupy their available time advising, mentoring, and counseling younger women in practical, hands-on ways about godly Christian womanhood, sound-mindedness, attitude, discretion, purity, kindness, marriage, childrearing, and stewardship of the home as listed in Titus 2:4–5. And obviously, women are the best to provide that practical teaching to other women.

Unfortunately, some women today are teaching the whole church rather than teaching just the ones God has assigned to them; namely, other women. They have decided that standing behind a pulpit in front of a mixed audience is where God has called them to serve, and they are comfortable teaching the Bible to men and women rather than focusing on Titus 2 principles for younger women.

How is there even room to diminish or ignore that women encouraging other women is a critical part of a healthy church? The Bible's mandate that women are not to teach or exercise authority over men (1 Tim 2:12) in no way belittles our value in the church, and that's because we have been given the unique role of being leaders in teaching and training other women.[4]

God's plan for His church is that women are to teach and train other women in the matters pertaining to our husbands, children and homes, along with our attitudes and behavior as uniquely female. But it doesn't stop there. As Paul continues his argument in 1 Timothy 2, he says, "Women will be preserved through the bearing of children if they continue in faith and love and sanctity with self-restraint" (v. 15). And how are we to learn

---

[4] I have included an appendix in the back of this book that further explains Paul's command of women not exercising authority over men.

how to continue in faith, love, and sanctity? It must be taught. We must be taught theology and doctrine. So, clearly, theology and doctrine are yet another area that women can be involved in the teaching and training of women in the church. Moreover, women ministering to other women naturally involves ministering to children and young people. Even if you are not married or don't have children or aren't able to have children of your own, you can still be involved in fulfilling the mandate of Titus 2. Ultimately, God has given women the opportunity for an expansive ministry, one that cannot be taken lightly just for the opportunity to teach and preach to men.

Just know and keep in mind that, whether married or single, fulfilling the Titus 2 mandate will not be easy. The role of women in the family has been undermined and under attack ever since Satan asked Eve the question, "Did God really say?" in the Garden of Eden. Today, there is an aggressive push to utterly desecrate any semblance of womanhood as God designed it. Make note of these statements from some well-known leaders of the feminist movement:

> By the year 2000 we will, I hope, raise our children to believe in human potential, not God. —Gloria Steinem[5]

> Since marriage constitutes slavery for women, it is clear that the Women's Movement must concentrate on attacking this institution. Freedom for women cannot be won without the abolition of marriage. —Sheila Cronin[6]

---

[5] Cited in John MacArthur, "God's Plan for Younger Women, Part 1" (March 7, 1993). Retrieved from https://www.gty.org/library/sermons-library/56-14/gods-plan-for-younger-women-part-.
[6] Ibid.

> In order to raise children with equality, we must take them away from families and communally raise them. — Dr. Mary Jo Bain[7]

> The most merciful thing a large family can do to one of its infant members is to kill it. —Margaret Sanger, founder of Planned Parenthood [8]

It is unfathomable that a woman would think in such ways, much less put on record and voice her true feelings. We're living in a time of all-out assault on women, marriage, and family. We're living in a time where women are being targeted and challenged to question their gender identity and sexual orientation. We're living in a time when women are encouraged to become whomever they want to become and love whomever they want to love.

Such perversion has made it so easy for women not to think twice about discarding their unborn babies. Although no threat to the mother's life, women are being told they have a right and duty to abort their babies up to the last trimester and even after giving birth, if she and her doctor believe it is best.

Women today are inundated with reality shows chronicling the everyday lives of female celebrities (some of whom are called "wives") and being led to aspire to a lifestyle that is in stark contrast to the Titus 2 woman. Being sensible, kind, and pure has all been hijacked by recklessness, severe hostility, and weak-mindedness. To the world, stewarding the home and being subject to your own husband is nothing more than a wasted life and a slave mentality from which you need to be set free. Couple that with pseudo-womanhood capturing the full attention of young women who feed off of what they see, believing that real women look and behave just like what is

---

[7] Ibid.

[8] Ibid.

portrayed on TV, social media, film, and stage, and the Titus 2 mandate can seem daunting. Older women may find themselves up against a seemingly impossible endeavor just to teach what the Bible says.

"So that the Word of God Will Not Be Dishonored"

Nonetheless, the Bible is clear about what the focus of our teaching should be. Loving your husband and children, being a worker at home, being sensible, pure, kind, and subject to your own husband—these are all highly important in the lives of Christian women! And if that is not convincing enough, Paul gives the reason why: "so that the Word of God will not be dishonored" (Titus 2:5).

The Word of God is on display, and it becomes cheapened and discredited when we as women downplay, misconstrue, disobey, or simply ignore the mandate of Titus 2 and its detailed instructions.

The Proverbs 31 Woman

I wonder if Paul had been reading Proverbs 31:10–31 when he penned the virtues of the Titus 2 woman. You can be certain that what he wanted the older women to teach the younger women was demonstrated in the Proverbs 31 woman's life.

The Proverbs 31 woman is often dismissed as unrealistic and unattainable. Numerous women tend to think no actual woman can live like her and do all of the things she did. I disagree with that notion! Although we live in a completely different time and culture, any woman who bows her knee and heart to the Lord God can be a Proverbs 31 woman in her culture and context.

It is obvious that King Lemuel's mother would also disagree with that notion. She seemed to me to be a serious, no-nonsense kind of woman. As King Lemuel recounts the things she taught him, we see that she warned her son about immorality and intemperance. She warned him about neglect and dereliction of duties. She urged her son to be the voice for those who had no voice. She fully believed there was an excellent woman for him, whose worth was far above rubies. Indeed, the question asked by her is an indication that this kind of woman does exist: An excellent wife, who can find? (Prov 31:10)

The wise woman builds her house.

The text of Proverbs 31 is not the only chapter in Proverbs that teaches us what it means to be a transformed woman of God. Numerous other Proverbs have a lot to say about God's expectation of any woman who "makes a claim to godliness" (1 Tim 2:10).

For instance, Proverbs 14 speaks volumes to every God-fearing woman, and much of what the older woman is to teach the younger women according to the specific instructions in Titus 2:3–5 can be understood from the actions of the Proverbs 14 woman: "The wise woman builds her house, But the foolish tears it down with her own hands" (Prov 14:1). The wise woman in this verse apparently loves her husband and children, which are the family that resides with her in the house. She has to be sensible in order to do the work necessary in building her house versus tearing it down. It is obvious that she is a worker at home and is subject to her own husband. In contrast, it is the foolish woman and the way she chooses to live that harms the Christian family and home, thus dishonoring and cheapening the Word of God (Titus 2:5).

Note that the wise woman is described as a builder. She is not building an edifice; she is building her home. How is she able to do that? Who is helping her? Just as in the physical building process there is an underwriter who assumes another party's financial risk, in the spiritual realm, there is also an underwriter. As the psalmist says, "Unless the Lord builds the house, they labor in vain who build it" (Ps 127:1).

In the life of the wise woman, God is her underwriter. God is the one who vouches for the building of her home. Her "building" must be done under the direction of and in conformity to the Lord's command, by his help and guidance. If it is not, she labors in vain. As she follows and obeys God's Word, He continues to underwrite her as she builds.

In fact, God is not just the underwriter, He is the builder also, according to Psalm 127:1. In other words, the wise woman's efforts in building her home must line up with His efforts. As her Lord builds, so does she.

The idea that the full-time wife, homemaker, and mother does not do significant work or is not productive unless she labors outside the context of her home, is laughable and ridiculous. In a culture that bases a woman's significance on whether she can out-career a man, the wise Proverbs 14 woman is a staggering example of a productive and laboring woman.

She is a sensible woman who looks well to the ways of her household and does not eat the bread of idleness. She is a woman expending energy in building her "house." That is, not a physical brick and mortar edifice, but rather she is building the lives of the people in the house. She owns what is hers and does not have a pattern of farming it out to another. Sure, she can hire a babysitter on occasion. But the best of herself and her time, talents, nurture, care, love and efforts are given to the people in her home. This is the normal pattern of a wise woman.

The building of a wise woman's home begins with her husband. Just as laying a good, solid foundation for a physical structure ensures the building will be stable, loving our husband God's way helps to ensure a stable, God-fearing family.

The wise woman loves her husband.

The first priority the older woman is to teach the younger woman according to Titus 2:4 is to love her husband. It may sound strange that love in a marriage relationship has to be taught. However, the emotionally tense rush two people may feel when dating and that Hollywood portrays as love, is not what is meant in that verse.

The Greek term for the word "love" used in this verse is *philos,* and for the word "husband" the Greek term is *andros.* When the two Greek words are put together, they form the compound word, *philandros,* which means "husband lover." What is to be understood is that a love of husband should be taught and developed in the younger woman's life. She needs to be encouraged to prioritize him in both her affections and actions. She needs to understand how to love him in a way that reflects total devotion to him.

How does a wife love her husband when she disagrees with a decision he has made? How does a wife love her husband when he is not the leader he ought to be? How does she love him when the marriage relationship becomes strained or turns sour? When frustrations and financial setbacks arise, along with a litany of other problems that can occur when two sinners are living under the same roof, loving our husbands can become difficult.

On the other hand, how does a wife love and show support to her husband as he provides for her and the family? As he endeavors to love, cherish, and lead her, how should her love for him manifest itself? Based on their years of firsthand experience, godly older women have a wealth of knowledge they can pass on to younger women in this area, as well. Faithfully loving their husbands through the high points and weathering the storms and rainy days of marriage takes a commitment and dedication that does not happen from an emotional rush or feelings of excitement and romance. The kind of love the Bible affirms does not come naturally and therefore requires teaching, training, time, and patience. In other words, a young woman will be learning how to love her husband throughout her marriage.

The wise woman submits to her husband.

Loving our husbands the way God intended requires submission and respect. Notice from the below Scripture that Paul exhorts the church of Ephesus on how a husband and wife are to conduct themselves in the marriage relationship. He begins his exhortation on the subject of submission and concludes on the subject of respect:

> Wives, be subject to your own husbands, as to the Lord. But as the church is subject to Christ, so also the wives

ought to be to their husbands in everything. . . . Nevertheless, each individual among you also is to Love his own wife even as himself, and the wife must see to it that she respects her husband. (Eph 5:22, 33)

The Greek word for "submission" is *hupotasso*, which means to arrange, to place, or to rank under. The Greek word for "respect" is *phobetai*, which means to reverence, venerate, or treat with deference. These two virtues are fundamental not only to the marriage relationship but also to the home-building process. The wise woman demonstrates her strength and ability to build her house in how she reigns herself in. She is not made or forced to submit but willingly places herself under the authority and leadership of her husband. She treats her husband with honor and reverence because her goal is to build according to her underwriter's (God's) wishes. The Bible is clear, submission to our husband is to be given "as to the Lord" and "in everything." While a woman can love her husband and not submit to him, she will not be loving him God's way.

Usually one of the first questions to be asked after hearing "in everything" is, "Do I have to submit if my husband ask me to do something wrong or to sin?" Submitting to your husband while at the same time disobeying God in another area is not submission. Remember, we are ultimately submitting to God's will. Acts 5:1–10 gives an excellent illustration of a woman who was asked to do something wrong by her husband. You know this to be the story of Ananias and Sapphira who "agreed together to put the Spirit of the Lord to the test" (v. 9).

Although Sapphira was in complete agreement with her husband and went along with him in the deceptive plot, this was not Christian submission but rather rebellion against God on her part. Instead of doing all things for the glory of God, she, like her husband, wanted the attention and accolades that would naturally come from the people. She was all about public perception. Her actions were not an expression of being in subjection to her husband as much as being equally deceptive and rebellious against God.

Yet, at first, God was gracious to Sapphira. Unlike her husband, God gave her more than one opportunity to disavow herself from the evil deed and to be truthful. Firstly, for whatever reason, she did not accompany Ananias when he brought the proceeds of the sale to the apostles. Perhaps that is due to God's providential grace, because if they both had been there and lied together, she probably would have collapsed and died on the spot just like he did.

Then, a period of three hours elapsed between the time Peter questioned Ananias and the time he questioned Sapphira. Where had she been for three hours? What was she doing while her husband was deceiving the church? The Bible does not say, but one thing is clear: God gave her that extra time to consider, or rather reconsider, what she and her husband had concocted. Interestingly, however, she was totally unaware that her husband had died as a direct result of his deception. Finally, Peter asked her specifically about the price of the land, giving her one last opportunity to be forthright. She still chose to lie, to her immediate demise.

The point of this example is that a *submissive* Christian wife would have been repulsed by such a plan hatched by her husband. She would have profoundly refused to conspire with him and perhaps would have even warned the church ahead of time about it.

Scripture is very clear. If we are married to a man who is disobedient to the Word, we are to continue to do the will of God regardless of how our husband behaves:

> In the same way, you wives, be submissive to your own husbands so that even if any of them are disobedient to the Word, they may be won without a word by the behavior of their wives, as they observe your chaste and respectful behavior. (1 Pet 3:1–2)

Sapphira should have rejected her husband's idea, confronted him (respectfully) over his sin and abandoned the plan. However, no sooner did the lie roll off her lips that she breathed her last breath and died. This is not Christian submission. This is not the actions of a woman being subject to her own husband. She was a co-conspirator in a fraud.

The example of the Proverbs 31 woman teaches every woman of God that loving her husband is summed up in doing "him good and not evil all the days of her life" (Prov 31:12). We can only imagine what might have been if only Sapphira had lived accordingly.

A wise woman loves her children.

John MacArthur has said:

> Generally speaking, women are mothers, and they are to bear children, and in bearing children they have then the responsibility to love those children. That means to sacrifice their life on the child's behalf. Again, the love is not an emotion. It's not standing in the corner gloating when your little child is all dressed up at how handsome or how beautiful she is. It is the responsibility of pouring your life sacrificially into that little life so that that child grows up to love Christ."[9]

Once again, it may sound strange that loving our children has to be taught. As mothers, we have a fierce commitment to our children and their wellbeing. We want to see them happy and thriving. Nothing hurts a mother more than seeing one of her children hurting. Our love for them is overwhelming and unending. When they are grown and have their own children, we love them just as much as we always have. Yet, the affection,

---

[9] John MacArthur, "God's Plan for Younger Women, Part 2" (March 14, 1993). Retrieved from https://www.gty.org/library/sermons-library/56-15/gods-plan-for-younger-women-part-2.

tenderness, and unconditional love we naturally have for them is not the sum total of what Titus 2:4 means when it tells us to love our children.

Children are a "gift from the Lord" (Ps 127:3) and are to be brought up in the fear and admonition of the Lord (Eph 6:4). They are to be trained in the way they should go, so that even when they are old, they will not depart (Prov 22:6). Although the last sentence is not a promise from God, it demonstrates where the focus and efforts of a loving mother should be.

As I stated earlier, the wise woman of Proverbs 14 builds her house; it's not a physical structure but the people who make up her house. She is constantly building the family up. Part of the building process is making sure every member of the home has the spiritual sustenance he or she needs, and that must include the children.

A wise woman knows what her children need spiritually because she is specifically marked by biblical wisdom. That is, strictly speaking, she is a woman informed by Scripture. She knows what the true, genuine, and lasting needs of mankind are, and she uses that knowledge to help build the lives of her children in the Lord. She eagerly takes on her role of loving her children in this way and channels her personal desires to this specific task, which has been given to her by her Lord. Teaching her children to know and love the Lord Jesus Christ is preeminent in how she loves her children. She strives to teach them to love God's Word and serve Him wholeheartedly. Through her own faithful commitment to the Lord, her children see modeled before them what being a child of God looks like.

The Proverbs 31 woman is very similar in how she builds her house. She knows that a vital part of looking well to the ways of her household includes the spiritual aspects of her family. The Word of God is central to her home, and her children are aware of it. As a result, they "rise up and bless her" (Prov 31:28).

A wise woman is sensible.

Proverbs 14 contrasts the wise woman with the foolish woman. The former builds and the latter tears down. You may get the idea that the text is describing two different women. However, consider with me that it may be referring to the same woman.

Perhaps the divinely inspired author wanted to demonstrate that each of us has the capacity to be foolish at any given time. Perhaps the author wanted the wise woman to realize what she needed to rigorously resist in her life. Perhaps he used the example of the foolish woman as a warning to women who desire to be sensible.

How did the foolish woman become foolish? There is no indication from the text that she planned to become foolish. She did not make it her goal in life to be a destructive person. She simply lived life the way she saw fit and devoid of divine influence.

Remember, the wise woman has God as her underwriter. She knows that she is only able to build because of Him. And as He builds, she builds. She is building in accordance with His standards and what pleases Him. In contrast, because she is so far removed from constructing, the foolish woman's efforts inevitably lead to destruction and ruin.

Below are some of the ways the Bible describes the foolish person in general:

To the foolish, God does not exist!	"The fool has said in his heart, 'There is no God.'" (Ps 14:1)
Fools don't care that injury to others may occur because of their words.	"A wise man is cautious and turns away from evil, but a fool is arrogant and careless." (Prov 14:16)

The fool is focused on other interests, totally oblivious that wisdom has evaded her.	"Wisdom is in the presence of the one who has understanding, but the eyes of a fool are on the ends of the earth." (Prov 17:24)
The fool has no desire to learn but only to air her opinions.[10]	"The fool does not delight in understanding, but only in revealing his own mind." (Prov 18:2)
The fool's behavior results in her own demise.	"The fool folds his hands and consumes his own flesh." (Eccl 4:5)
The fool is easily identifiable because she is easily angered.	"Do not be eager in your heart to be angry, for anger resides in the bosom of fools." (Eccl 7:9)

Next, I want you to notice the many ways being sensible benefitted the family of the Proverbs 31 woman. From Proverbs 31:10–31 you'll see that:

- Her husband had no lack of gain. (v. 11)
- She was concerned about quality in meeting the needs of her family, not just things that looked pretty. (vv. 13, 21, 22)
- Her focus was not on filling an empty stomach but on providing the best nutrient-dense foods available. (v. 14)
- After careful consideration, she purchased land that would enhance her home and prosper her family. (v. 16)
- She refused to shy away from hard, laborious work. (vv. 17–18)

---

[10] Ryrie, *Study Bible*, 993.

- She developed a skill that allowed her to earn income but did not overshadow her household responsibilities. (v. 24)
- She knew when to open her mouth and what was appropriate to say. (v. 26)
- She did not give the best of her time, energy, and efforts to things that took her away from her household. (v. 27)
- Because she feared the Lord, she handled her responsibilities with excellence for His glory. (v. 30)

The wise woman is pure and kind.

The Greek word for "pure" is *hagnas*, which means chaste, morally pure and virtuous. While kindness can be seen, experienced, and expressed, purity is somewhat obscure. We can behave in a certain way that reflects kindness, benevolence, and overall goodwill towards others, but only God knows if our intentions are truly pure. Only God knows our heart.

Therefore, if purity and true, genuine kindness are to radiate from our lives, there must be a focus on inward adornment. That's why God specifically says to women:

> Your adornment must not be merely external, braiding the hair, and wearing gold jewelry, or putting on dresses; but let it be the hidden person of the heart, with the imperishable quality of a gentle and quiet spirit, which is precious in the sight of God. (1 Pet 3:3–4)

> I want women to adorn themselves with proper clothing, modestly and discreetly, not with braided hair and gold or pearls or costly garments, but rather by means of good works, as is proper for women making a claim to godliness. (1 Tim 2:9–10)

The internal landscape of a woman's heart must be drastically altered if purity and kindness will flow from it. Her internal landscape must be first and foremost impacted by the Word of God, developing a meek and quiet spirit, modesty and discretion in outward appearance, and pursuing good works.

Dear Sis

As I said, operating by the Titus 2 mandate for women (Titus 2:3–5) is a daunting task, but also recall that there is a good reason for it: "So that the word of God will not be dishonored" (Titus 2:5). To dishonor or malign the Word of God is a severe matter. The word translated "malign" is *blasphemeo*, from which we get our English word *blaspheme*. *Blasphemeo* means to defame, to speak evilly or profanely of sacred things.

You have heard the saying, "Actions speak louder than words." Maligning, dishonoring, blaspheming the Word of God is something we attribute to the actions of Satan and the lost souls of this world. But when we fail to love our husband and children and neglect our home, we are also maligning and dishonoring the Word of God. When we ignore our role of submission, act in an unkind manner, and live an impure and foolish life, we are maligning the Word of God. Even when we fail to teach, train or give good advice to younger women, we are potentially maligning the Word of God

By our actions and behavior, we can cause others to be either drawn to the Word or repelled from it. We either validate God's Word or invalidate it. Who will take seriously a book that has been maligned by the very people who claim to love and obey it? Who will take seriously a gospel that has been cheapened by the very people who say they have faith in it? This was Paul's point when he said, "so that the opponent will be put to shame, having nothing bad to say about us" (Titus 2:8).

Sister, we have been given a significant and sacred responsibility. Our willing, joyful, and eager obedience to the will of God makes the Word of

God attractive to the lost and the disobedient. As we faithfully obey, we take part in adorning "the doctrine of God our Savior in every respect" (Titus 2:10).

The world continues to boldly communicate their views of what women should look like and act like, what they should do with "their own bodies," and that their number one priority should be breaking glass ceilings. But the decision every woman is compelled to make is, *Am I going to follow the world or follow the Word?* If we are truly transformed, the only answer is to follow the Word. My prayer is that this is your heartbeat as a transformed woman of God.

What Are Your Thoughts?

1. What stood out to you or caused you to raise an eyebrow in this chapter?

2. What is the greatest hindrance to becoming Titus 2 women in our culture today?

3. What are the top three struggles for most Christian women in obeying the Titus 2 mandate?

4. How can culture distract or entice Christian women away for fulfilling the Titus 2 mandate? In your discussion, consider educational accomplishments, career advancement, and the media/social media.

5. Some pastors teach and some women believe that Paul's commands in 1 Timothy 2:11–12 and Ephesians 5:22, 24 and 33 are solely based on the culture in which he lived. How would you argue against this position?

6. How does reading, studying, meditating on, and memorizing Scripture also help safeguard us from maligning God's Word?

7. The Proverbs 31 woman was not a real estate broker, as some have erroneously thought. Purchasing a piece of land does not make you a real estate broker any more than administering medicine to your child makes you a doctor. Make a list of things that a sensible woman will take into consideration before making a purchase of this magnitude.

8. What did you notice about the Proverbs 31 woman's disposition in handling her responsibilities? What can we learn from her example?

On a Personal Note

From the example of the Proverbs 31 woman, what character trait(s) do you desire to see developed in your own life? What steps will you take in seeking to grow in those areas?

APPENDIX
Three Reasons the Pulpit is No Place for Women

Fifty years ago, there were virtually no women leading congregations as pastors in America except in a few Pentecostal and a handful of mainline churches. In 1960, sociologist Wilbur Bock combed U.S. census data to learn that women were 2.3% of U.S. clergy, but not all of them were pastors. Then, in the 1970s, growth in women's ordination exploded and continued to rise steadily through the next four decades. By 2014, women constituted 15.8% of clergy in America, and they led 10% of U.S. congregations. In 2016 the American Communities Survey census data reported that women were 20.7% of professional clergy in the United States.[1]

More ink has been spilled over the subject of women being allowed to pastor, preach, and hold leadership positions in the Christian church, and it continues to be an ever-present point of contention. Not nearly as much writing has been done on the Proverbs 31 or Titus 2 woman. Why is that?

---

[1] Eileen Campbell-Reed, "State of Clergywomen in the U.S.: A Statistical Report" (October 2018). Retrieved from https://eileencampbellreed.org/wp-content/uploads/Downloads/State-of-Clergywomen-US-2018-web.pdf.

Why is there so much debate, discussion, and disagreement over the roles of women in the church? That question may never be answered.

That doesn't change the fact that the Bible is very clear that female pastors are prohibited. Here are three reasons why from the Scriptures:

Reason One: Women are not allowed to teach or exercise authority over men.

> A woman must quietly receive instruction with entire submissiveness. But I do not allow a woman to teach or exercise authority over a man, but to remain quiet. For it was Adam who was first created, and then Eve. And it was not Adam who was deceived, but the woman being deceived, fell into transgression. (1 Tim 2:11–14)

Women were never given the role and responsibility of teaching or shepherding the church. It was given exclusively to qualified men (1 Tim 3:1–7). Paul explains why this was the case by referencing the events of Creation. It was not because women are less than men or unable to lead, but because God created Adam before He created Eve.

He gave Adam a job and instructions on what he was expected to do in the Garden of Eden. Those instructions were to be communicated to Eve once she was created. Through the creation process, God established a hierarchy of position whereby Adam was made the head of the home and leader of his family, and Eve was to support him in that role.

God wanted the same for His Church. In the corporate gathering of the church, men are to be the leaders and to give spiritual oversight to all of the members. Although some women have been given the gift of teaching just like men, their teaching is not to be facilitated to men. God has reserved the biblical learning of men to be provided by other men.

This prohibition has nothing to do with a woman's skill or ability to understand and explain the Scriptures. It has everything to do with God's order and the way He wants His church to function. Also keep in mind, men were never commanded not to teach or exercise authority over women.

If a woman has a desire to preach, it was not given to her by God. A desire is not necessarily a calling. Some women believe that if they are under the "covering" of their husband or under the authority of their local church leaders, they are free to teach the Bible to a mixed audience. What does it mean to be under the covering of your husband? Where is that mentioned in the Scriptures?

Besides, if this were true, we would have to believe that God allows the very leadership He established to overrule *Him* in certain situations. Which is basically usurping His authority, which no man or woman ever has the right to do. So, husbands, pastors, and church leaders do not have the authority to supersede God's commands!

As was stated earlier in this book, a transformed woman of God does not use her pastor or her husband in order to function in a role contrary to God's clearly expressed will for her.

Reason Two: A woman cannot be the *husband* of one *wife*.

> If any man aspires to the office of overseer, it is a fine work he desires to do. An overseer, then, must be above reproach, the husband of one wife ... He must be one who manages his own household well, keeping his children under control with all dignity, but if a man does not know how to manage his own household, how will he take care of the church of God? (1 Tim 3:1–2a)

Paul gives specific qualifications for the one who desires to pastor and have spiritual oversight of a body of believers. First, Paul states that the individual must be the husband of one wife. A husband is a man. A woman can never be a husband. Contrary to the gender dysphoria foolishness occurring in our culture today, women are not men and never will be. Only men were created to become husbands. As such, the husband is held accountable by God to be the spiritual head and leader of his wife just as Christ is the head and leader of the church (Eph 5:25–29).

Also, notice how Paul appeals to God's order. The one desiring to be an overseer is not only to be the husband of one wife, but he must also manage his own household well. It makes no sense for a man to attempt to oversee and manage the church family when he is unable to manage his own family.

Remember what took place in the Garden of Eden. God created Adam and "put him in the garden of Eden to cultivate it and keep it" (Gen 2:7, 15). Next, the Lord commanded the man not to eat from the tree of the knowledge of good and evil. All of these events took place before Eve was created.

When God created Eve, He gave her no instructions. He simply "brought her to the man" (Gen 2:22). How was she to find out what God had commanded? God's expectation was that Adam, as head of his home, would inform her.

God established order in the home and submitted to His own order when He created Eve. Rather than instructing her directly, He allowed her husband, Adam, to communicate to his wife about the tree that was off-limits.

A wife's responsibility is to submit to her husband in everything as she does to the Lord (Eph 5:22–24). Paul also states that women originated from men, as evidenced by God creating Eve from one of Adam's ribs. That act has significant ramifications. The question, then, that begs to be asked is, why did He create man and woman in that manner? Why not create both simultaneously? Why the delay in creating the woman? The answer is simple: The woman was created not only *from* the man but also *for* the man (Gen 2:18, 1 Cor 11:9).

It is unfortunate that these truths ignite such a firestorm of controversy even among Christian women. In the broader culture, even in churches, they may even be considered hate speech towards women.

Reason Three: A woman preaching and teaching the body of Christ is distracted from fulfilling the mandate of Titus 2.

> Older women likewise are to be reverent in their behavior, not malicious gossips nor enslaved to much wine, teaching what is good, so that they may encourage the young women to love their husbands, to love their children, to be sensible, pure, workers at home, kind, being subject to their own husbands, so that the word of God will not be dishonored. (Titus 2:3–5)

God has given women a unique role as His image bearers. We reflect Him and His beautiful plan best when we function within that role. The specific attributes of that role include the following:

- We are life-givers. (Gen 3:20)
- We are a helper suitable to our husband. (Gen 2:18)
- We are the glory of man. (1 Cor 11:7)
- We are builders; we build up our homes. (Prov 14:1)
- We look well to the ways of our household. (Prov 31:27)
- We open our mouths in wisdom. (Prov 31:26)
- We extend our hand to the poor. (Prov 31:20)
- We are industrious. (Prov 31:16)
- We treat our husbands well all the days of our life. (Prov 31:12)
- We are excellent. (Prov 31:10)

Endeavoring to live godly lives and to teach each other things pertaining specifically to the mandate of Titus 2 so that the word of God is not dishonored is what we are clearly and directly called to do by God. As such, it is where our obedience to His true calling on us as women, can be most effective in protecting His Word from being maligned.

www.ingramcontent.com/pod-product-compliance
Lightning Source LLC
Chambersburg PA
CBHW071002160426
43193CB00012B/1878